Through High Windows

Georg Sauter, *Portrait of Lilian Sauter*, 1911,
oil on canvas, 71.1 x 55.9 cm
Courtesy of and ©Research and Cultural Collections,
University of Birmingham.

LILIAN SAUTER

Through High Windows
and Other Writings

Edited with a critical introduction by Jeffrey S. Reznick

Universitas Press
Montreal

Universitas Press
Montreal

U

www.universitaspress.com

First published in July 2025

Library and Archives Canada Cataloguing in Publication

Title: Through high windows and other writings / Lilian Sauter ;
edited with a critical
    introduction by Jeffrey S. Reznick.
Names: Sauter, Lilian, author. | Container of (work): Sauter, Lilian.
Through high windows. |
    Reznick, Jeffrey S. (Jeffrey Stephen), editor, writer of
introduction.
Identifiers: Canadiana 20250205246 | ISBN 9781998579006
(hardcover)
Subjects: LCSH: Sauter, Lilian. | LCSH: English poetry—20th
century—Criticism and interpretation. |
    LCGFT: Poetry.
Classification: LCC PR6037.A864 T47 2025 | DDC 821/.912—
dc23

Contents

Figures

Acknowledgements

This book grew from my previous research on Lilian Sauter's son, Rudolf, the artist and poet, and her brother, John, the Nobel Prize-winning author of *The Forsyte Saga*. As Rudolf lived in the shadow his famous uncle and deserved his unique story being told, so did Lilian with respect of her own meaningful life and experiences. To this end, I revisited her 1911 book *Through High Windows* as a focus and framework, understanding that the copyright therein is now in the public domain according to UK copyright law which dictates that such copyright remains in effect from the date of creation of works until seventy years following the author's death. I was also motivated to research and write about Lilian by a fact all historians can appreciate: here was an interesting, understudied, and undervalued story which deserved to be told using a variety of ignored and underappreciated archival and published sources. In this regard, I thank Cristina Artenie, Dragos Moraru, and Declan Murdoch of Universitas Press for their valuable time, supportive expertise, generous enthusiasm, and willingness to work together to bring this book to fruition.

I am equally grateful to many individuals who dedicated their time and expertise to helping me complete this book. I would especially like to thank Susan Worrall, Director of the Cadbury Research Library, University of Birmingham, for permission to reproduce Lilian's unpublished writings and related materials held there, along with the fine team of the library for their generous support, including Megan Ashworth, Hamda Gharib, Asma Iftikhar, Martin Killeen, Philip Tromans, and Mark Williams.

The University of Delaware Libraries holds a significant collection of Lilian's papers, including poems dedicated to her friend Frieda and to her daughter-in-law Viola, as well as an original copy of *Through High Windows* which she inscribed to her husband Georg. I am deeply grateful to Mark Samuels Lasner and Valerie Stenner for permission to reproduce portions of these materials in this book and welcoming me to study the collection with my daughter, Danielle. It was her first time experiencing the richness of a university special collection, and it was a wonderful occasion for her, and for both of us.

I also thank many more knowledgeable and generous individuals for their time and expertise, including Valeria Carullo, RIBA British Architectural Library; Carolynne Cotton and Amy Graham, Kingston Heritage Service; Renée Cuthbert and the team at the National

Institutes of Health Library; Claire Freston, Highgate Cemetery; Elizabeth Garver, Harry Ransom Canter, The University of Texas at Austin; Elizabeth Goodacre and Madeleine Goodall, Humanists UK; Amy Graham and colleagues at the Kingston History Centre; Stephen Greenberg, John Rees, and Ginny Roth, National Library of Medicine (NLM); Liz Howlett, Jeremy Jay, and The Othona Community, West Dorset; Jenny Lance, Research and Cultural Collections, University of Birmingham; Matthew Neill and Mariam Yamim, Special Collections, Heritage, and Archives, University of Sheffield, Western Bank Library, and Dane Williams, University of Montana.

Moreover, I am grateful to Kristina Dunne for her careful transcription of Lilian's work as part of her many fine accomplishments as a Pathways intern at the NLM; Krista Stracka, also at the NLM, for her expertise in the anatomy of rare books; Nalina Gopal for her valuable time and fabulous research expertise, as well as Margot Finn for connecting us; and Mair Salts for traveling to Highgate Cemetery and photographing Lilian's resting place there in cooperation with Claire Freston.

Finally, I am grateful to Linda Watson and her colleagues at Transcription Services Ltd., and to my NLM colleague Jim Labosier, for their expertise in deciphering instances of Lilian's most challenging handwriting.

I appreciate the institutional support I received during my research and writing of this book as part of my official duties as a historian employed by the United States Federal Government at the NLM. None of the opinions presented here represent the views of the NLM. According to Section 105 of the United States Copyright Act, the intellectual work I produce through my official duties belongs to the United States Federal Government and is not subject to copyright within the United States. Therefore, I cannot claim the copyright in portions of this book which I have authored and neither can I transfer any copyright nor accept any royalties. As my public service advances the greater good, so does this book through its copyright status. Any errors in the text are my own, and I will appreciate hearing from anyone who would contact me with corrections.

I dedicate this book to Lilian in respect of her voice and experiences in her time, and to my wife, Allison, and daughters, Danielle and Rachel, in respect of their voices and experiences in our time.

Introduction

Through High Windows is "a little book worth reading." So declared *The Poetry Review* in May 1912 about the recently published collection of poetry by Lilian Sauter (*"Through High Windows"* 234). The same declaration inspires this new edition of her book. The mere forty pages of *Through High Windows*, containing twenty-two poems, belies its historical value as a focus and framework to study her intriguing life and contextualize a selection of her unpublished writings.

Scholars have recognized Lilian as a sister of the noted British author John Galsworthy (1867-1933), the mother of the artist and poet Rudolf Helmut Sauter (1895-1977), and the wife of the distinguished painter Georg Sauter (1866-1937). The time has come to appreciate her in her own right, as the poet, suffragist, and creative figure her contemporaries recognized her to be, in ways biographers have either ignored or underappreciated.

As Lilian's only book, *Through High Windows* represented the culmination of her publishing achievements and a pinnacle of her lifelong interest in conveying the beauty of the natural world. Herein she also reflected deeply on her personal relationships and offered commentary on the issue of women's suffrage. The text of the entire book appears below in modern font and with periodic footnotes highlighting facts and brief background—all connected to this introduction—to help readers understand and appreciate Lilian's work in context. A century after her passing, therefore, this book locates Lilian in a story of her own. It reveals her multifaced life filled with curiosity about interior and exterior worlds, friendship and love, and sociability and political advocacy, particularly in association with other women of her time who, like Lilian, are not as known and appreciated as they should be. Read in conjunction with her unpublished work, this introduction is intended to be enlightening, not comprehensive, to inspire further study of her activities, associations, and experiences breaking through lingering Victorian separate spheres, to live and grow in the public domain and participate in its prevailing ethic of work and achievement.

Biography and Character

Blanche Lilian Galsworthy [Figure 1] was born in Marylebone, London, on September 1, 1864, to John Galsworthy (1817-1904), a wealthy solicitor, and his wife, Blanche Bailey (Bartleet) (1837-1915). Known by her family and friends as Lilian, or Lily, she would become the eldest of four siblings, including brothers John and Hubert, born 1867 and 1869, respectively, and sister Mabel Edith, born 1871 [Figure 2]. The family lived in a prosperous upper-middle-class household located in Kingston on Thames (Marrot 55ff).

Decades after Lilian's passing, Mabel recalled her as "quiet and studious...[a] rare spirit in a frail body...who brought to us three younger ones the greater part of such mental stimulus as our very normal, ordinary lives ever knew. Always quietly busy herself with her painting, reading, needlework, or writing, it was she who would start interesting subjects for discussion; she who told us stories when we were little; she who opened our eyes and minds to beautiful things to be seen or heard or read" (Reynolds 17). Lilian's cousin Muriel similarly recalled her intelligence—she "had Uncle Jack's brain with an added quickness Jack didn't have"—while her distant cousin Dorothy Ivens recalled her as "never selfish...unconventional" and an individual who "really loved people" (Gindin, *The English Climate* 161).

Figure 1
Cabinet card depicting Blanche Lilian Sauter, ca. early 1880s, during the period of her unpublished writings which appear in this book.
Courtesy of Cadbury Research Library: Special Collections, University of Birmingham, JG(II)/10/8.

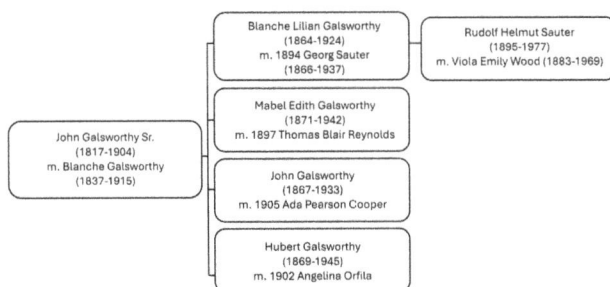

Figure 2
Lilian Sauter family tree, abridged to include key individuals mentioned in this book.
Diagram created by the author.

By the 1880s, as the sisters' friend Agnes Sanderson recalled, the pair "had grown into two intelligent and thoughtful young women" who, "had they been born fifty years later," would

most certainly have graduated from Girton or Somerville. To their own generation these young intellectuals were almost alarming. At first we were nervous of them. They were well educated and very 'Arty.' They wore at that time immense beaver hats with ostrich feathers drooping on to their shoulders. Long seal-skin coats enveloped their small figures, and the effect was unfamiliar to us. They scarcely spoke above a whisper, and were very serious. They were good linguists, and never used slang (Dupré 31-32).

Sanderson concluded that "if not conventionally beautiful, Lilian and Mabel were extremely attractive girls: Lily like a moth, so tiny and gentle, the other Mable, more like [their brother] Jack [i.e., John], but with the most marvellous golden hair" (Dupré 31-32).

In his own recollections, Lilian's son Rudolf described her as "a person of great selflessness, to come into contact with whom was like crossing the frontier into another world, in which the values of currency had been mysteriously transmuted into something other than those negotiable in ordinary life. Everybody loved her, with her slight figure which any wind might blow away, her halo of grey hair, her serious smile, her beautiful grey eyes and her loving nature, small and delicate, she was able to unlock most hearts." Rudolf also recalled that his mother's frailty was a lifelong condition due to a number of ailments, including scoliosis (Rudolf Sauter 35).

Biographers of Lilian's famous brother John contribute to this portrait of her character in important but limited ways. Dudley Barker observed that she, "with her intensity, her sensitive intellect and her consuming desire to be a poet, devoted herself, perhaps without too much discrimination, to contemporary art, particularly to literature"

(31). Catherine Dupré offered that Lilian was "exceptionally small in build" and "gave the appearance of being a fragile and delicate person." Dupré wrote further that "such an impression would be misleading. She was a person of extraordinary character and will-power, and of quite outstanding intellectual ability. She had too a gentle and sympathetic nature, and an ability to communicate with those with whom she came into contact" (20-21). James Gindin also documented Lilian's intellect by pointing out that in the Galsworthy home during the 1880s, she "was the leader in all serious conversation, concentrating on her always receptive brother Jack, even as early as his graduation from Harrow, in 1886, when she wrote telling him how proud she and everyone else was of his fine speech, but added a number of suggestions to give his public speaking greater range and effectiveness" (Gindin, *Life and Art* 47). Additionally, Gindin noted a similar example dating from the summer of 1888, when Lilian and John "were reading Matthew Arnold's 'Literature and Dogma' and studying Emerson...leading to long and thorough discussions about Christianity and other religions, and [the pair] arriving at a position of scepticism and agnosticism that neither ever substantially altered" (Gindin, *Life and Art* 47). Harold Vincent Marrot likewise pointed out that Lilian and John were similarly minded, she with a desire to learn and create which would drive her to be "ferociously literary" and, along with John, to rebel against the older generation and reject conventional Christian teachings (Marrot 108-109, 120; Dupré 33). Marrot further acknowledged that evidence of Lilian's literary interest may be found in her diaries which reveal that as early as 1892, she discussed with John a book she was thinking about writing (Cadbury Library, JG(II)/10/1). Additional evidence may be found in the fact that she suggested "alterations" to John's 1900 novel *Villa Rubein*, a story about "the love of a young Austrian painter for an English girl" which was inspired by and dedicated to Lilian and her husband Georg, whom she had married in 1894 (Marrot 109, 120; Barker 69, 80-81). Finally, Ralph Hale Mottram mentioned but failed to elaborate on the fact that, by 1907, Lilian began to establish her reputation as a socially conscious author (29).

This limited portrait of Lilian, constructed through fleeting recollections and biographies of her brother, points to how and why she is deserving of a spotlight, to illuminate her own ideas, interests, inquisitiveness, and expressions of creativity. Indeed, who was Lilian on her own terms? The written and visual records of her thoughts and experiences—in diaries, journals, letters, sketchbooks, and miscellaneous personal papers—combined with contemporary images and published sources, offer answers to this question, revealing her life of introspection around subjects of philosophy, nature, and religion. In turn, this perspective reflects Lilian's enthusiastic and independent participation in the traditionally masculine life of the mind, rejection of the separate feminine sphere, and early development of suffragist views.

Early Life and Writings

Coombe, Surrey

By 1881, when Lilian was seventeen years old, she and her family had moved from Kingston upon Thames to Coombe, Surrey, where her father built three large homes on the estate formerly owned by the Duke of Cambridge: Coombe Warren, Coombe Leigh, and Coombe Croft. During various periods from the late 1860s through the early 1880s, the Galsworthy family lived in all three of these residences. A ceremonial artifact of the period reveals through its engraving that young Lilian "laid the foundation stone" of Coombe Warren, while the house itself later inspired her brother's creation of Robin Hill in his trilogy *The Forsyte Saga* [Figure 3]. In relegating the narrative of Lilian's life to John's, this object obscures what her contemporary writings make clear: Lilian herself found substantial creative and intellectual inspiration in and around each of these homes, particularly Coombe Leigh and Coombe Croft [Figures 4 and 5]. These writings, in turn, became the foundation upon which she grew her curiosity, creativity, independence, and abilities to capture her perspectives and experiences in poetic form.

Figure 3

Photograph of a commemorative heart-shaped trowel which Lilian used to lay the foundation stone of Coombe Warren. It is inscribed: "In 1867, with this trowel, Blanche Lilian Galsworthy aged 3 laid the foundation stone of Coombe Warren House, Surrey, lived in by John Galsworthy her father and his family. It suggested to her brother John Galsworthy the *Forsyte Saga*'s 'Robin Hill.'" Courtesy of and ©Research and Cultural Collections, University of Birmingham.

Figure 4
Image depicting Coombe Leigh, ca. 1885-6, from *The Garden: An Illustrated Weekly Journal of Gardening in All Its Branches* 29, January 30, 1886, p 89. Courtesy of the University of Massachusetts Amherst via HathiTrust.

Figure 5
Cabinet card depicting Coombe Croft, September 1885.
Collection and courtesy of the author.

Lilian's earliest writings, composed in and around Coombe Leigh and Coombe Croft, date from approximately 1881 to 1883. These include "Begun New Year's Eve," a reflection on the year soon past and the new one to come, and "Very Early Fragment," her contemplation of the sun, birds, breeze, trees, and "distant chimes" which "come floating softly." In "Fragment," composed as part of an evening poetry game held in Coombe Leigh, Lilian reflected on her choice of the word "forest," in response to the question "which talent do you most admire?" She used the word to create actions and imagery of a "forest king" in order to convey her "uncarried out idea being able to make spirits arise from the stream & pass before him each representing a talent, from which he was to choose the loveliest." Also standing among Lilian's early writings, dating from approximately 1885 to 1887 and composed in Coombe and various other locations, are a variety of "lines" which she dedicated to her sister, father, and mother, and to her friend Helene, whose surname is unknown; poems which she either composed for or signed with "Châtelaine" ("lady of the house"), and reflections on locales where her father rented large country houses for extended family outings, including Ashburton, Dartmoor, Devon, Teignmouth, and Torquay (Cadbury Library, JG(II)/10/6; Dupré 31).

Kensington Palace Mansions, London

Lilian and her family relocated to London in the mid-1880s, a change which "was chiefly in order that Lily might be within reach of the lectures and concerts she wanted to attend" (Reynolds 22). During this period, and mainly when they had settled in Kensington Palace Mansions, Lilian wrote extensively in her notebooks, contemplating her external and internal worlds. Among her efforts in the former category was her "first sonnet," which she dedicated to her friend Helene. She also composed "1st & last experience of the upper gallery," a reflection on the "exceptionally crowded audiences" during an orchestral concert in St. James's Hall led by the eminent German conductor Hans Richter who was introducing "the British public to the then unknown symphonic poems of Liszt, the symphonies of Brahms, and large extracts of Wagner's operas" (Kitson 381).

Lilian explored her internal world through various works in her personal journals, including an essay entitled "Thoughts on the Atonement" (November 1886), reflections on the work of contemporary religious thinkers in (spring 1887), another essay entitled "The Ethics of Truth" (May 1887), and—included below among other unpublished poems—"Thoughts of a Cartesian Sceptic" (ca. May 1887). She began the first of these compositions by quoting Genesis 2:17: "'In the day that thou eatest [from the tree of knowledge] thereof thou shalt surely die.'" Herein, she asked "What kind of death – ? What was man's sinless life? An eternal bodily life; was this present body to undergo no change, save the gradual natural development & the realisation from constant subjection to higher Will." She concluded, "I do not think so," explaining that

> Death seems to be a primary law of GOD's Material creation, as sure, as good, as the law of birth, wherever there is development, progress, there is death. It is the grand

evolution of GOD's world of beautiful Nature from life to death from death to life! It is as the painting of the [great] World-heart of GOD – life death, life death. Therein is His Divine economy, thereby every atom of matter is fitted into the World-organisation & finds its perpetual use. And therein we see as in the spiritual World the law of self sacrifice; unconsciously carried out, but not unconsciously designed. Leaf, flower, grain, & things of higher life, die only to live again in other forms, death is only change not annihilation; & it was from the beginning, it is a good thing & not an evil, consequent on sin & man's body partakes of the nature of all flesh, it grows, it wears away, it is daily dying & living again in other forms, the very fact of man's birth is an earnest of his death, what has a beginning must have an end, in nature; the World too, would be vastly overpeopled were there births & no deaths. No – we cannot separate man from the rest of matter, or say that GOD's laws for matter are evil (Cadbury Library, JG(II)/10/2/1).

She continued:

Bodily death then is not meant in that threat. We see this again on looking at GOD's ideal of Man. Christ was preordained of Him before foundation of World, & Christ died bodily now it seems to me that His Life & death existed from eternity in GOD's Mind as the perfect ideal of humanity, & not as a necessary outcome of the sin of man; That GOD intended man to be & do like Christ, from the first, & did not ordain that Christ should die because He knew that man was going to sin, & it was the only remedy or make-shift possible. I think we cannot imagine that if man had never sinned, & had been like Christ, he would have differed from Him in this respect. Christ has shown that bodily death is not an evil; but a welcome change, for beautiful as the pure sinless body of unfallen man would have been, yet the Soul must necessarily be freer disunited from it (Cadbury Library, JG(II)/10/2/1).

Connected to these compositions were Lilian's reflections on the work of two contemporary religious thinkers, Alfred Williams Momerie (1848-1900), an English cleric and academic of Broad Church views, and Alfred Edersheim (1825-1889), a Jewish convert to Christianity who was known especially for his 1883 book *The Life and Times of Jesus the Messiah*.

"'You have very unusual metaphysical power,'" Lilian quoted Momerie in her journal entry of March 12, 1887. "'I hope you will read a good deal, & afterwards write, on metaphysical subjects. Minds like yours—with a metaphysical bent are much needed in the present day."' Suggesting that she had corresponded directly with him, Lilian explained that "these words have come to me from Dr. Momerie himself with the stimulating, vivifying power of a call from Heaven. Bringing with them such a mysterious, exquisite pleasure as no praise has ever brought me hitherto; & a sense, transient, but how doubly delightful, of confidence in self, the true self, akin to GOD." His words, she explained further, "are a revelation of myself to me. In some degree the effect of them may be compared to the overwhelming effect of that glorious burst of "Light" in the opening of the 1st day in Haydn's *Creation*. It is indescribable."

A few days later, Lilian reflected on the work of Edersheim, explaining that he offered the "def[inition] of dif[ference] between Christ[ianity] & heathenism; latter idealisation of the visible, trying to carry earth into Heaven. [F]ormer realisation of the invisible, or bringing Heaven upon earth." She concluded her thoughts: "Greatest of all miracles, the condescension of Christ to men, & next to it, ascension of a slave, to Christ."

In "The Ethics of Truth," which constituted "notes for a discussion" at a Lexham Gardens residence which she had visited in May 1887, Lilian set out to explore "What is Truth." She began by quoting John 18:38: "Truth metaphysically defined would be—harmony of knowledge with fact. Truth is 2-sided. 1 objective 2 subjective but as the objective is to us [is] meaningless without the subjective, it is, as far as concerns us only definable as above." She wrote further that "Truth is ethically regarded may be defined as harmony of expression with knowledge (expression being taken in its broadest extension). This harmony, in the absolute is the basis of moral law—an approximation thereto a primary duty of every moral being." She continued:

> In the consideration of the practical working of this fundamental principle, we are confronted with a great difficulty, viz: that in obeying the laws of truth we are occasionally obliged to infringe the law of love (kindness, consideration) & other laws. How is it that these 2 fundamental ethical laws clash, & how are they to be reconciled? I think an answer is to be found in close consideration of the nature of truth. Truth is of various kinds & degrees of importance, roughly of 3 kinds:
>
> 1. harmony of carnal knowledge (i.e., the natural impulses & desires which are mostly intuitions or inherited inferences) with expression, e.g. my eating what I know will be good for me.
>
> 2. harmony of inferential knowledge with expression e.g. my correct statement of a scientific fact, or of my political opinions.
>
> 3. harmony of my moral or spiritual nature with my actions.

Lilian considered further that:

Perfect truth (ethically) would be the perfect harmony of my entire nature with itself & its every manifestation. The highest part of my nature is the spiritual, or rather the highest object of my knowledge is the right & good. Therefore, when I have realised that love, is the fulfilling of the law, the supreme good, in acting upon that knowledge, in expressing that feeling of love, which reason and intuition tells me is the highest feeling in my nature, I am being true to my highest self, i.e. to GOD. If in order to do this I am obliged to 'tell a lie' i.e. be untrue to my intellectual nature, I am not therefore sacrificing truth to love, but a low to a high kind of truth. So I am often truest in being most untrue (in the popular sense).

As for the "laws of truth & love," she wrote further, they

are not two laws which clash, but only a high & low development or rather application of the same, the one great, moral law of truth. With a nature complex, & self divided as ours, it is impossible to be true to all parts at once, manifestly if true to the higher we are untrue to our and opposing impulses, & again if two parts of our nature could be expressed at once from their agreement, still, owing to our imperfect organism or the imperfect moral nature of others, only one could be expressed at a time.

Moreover, she explained, regarding "the difficulty when we consider the casuistry of Truth is, not, to discern which duty is outwardly most binding & whether sacrificing one to the other be a sin, but

to judge which part of my nature of the two or more which claim allegiance from action, is the highest, & whether I can be true to more than one. The highest truth of which I am capable tho' entailing untruth to impulse which put in a minor claim, gathers it up into itself & transmits it, by the power of its motive, into right. I hold it to be the motive & not the end, which justifies the deed.

Lilian argued even further that

These two are not the same thing! A doctor would e.g. be justified in telling a lie if on that lie depended the chance recovery of his patient but it would not be the end, excellent tho' it might be which justified him but the love which prompted his effort for the recovery. If his sole aim [were], thro' the cure his self-aggrandisement, his lie would not be justifiable, his evil motive would work moral decay, his lie would have done him harm not being counter-balanced by right feeling; tho' the immediate object of it were the same.

xviii

And she concluded, yet ending her final thoughts as "unfinished":
The justification of a sin, means the prevention of its reflex evil effect on the character of him who commits it. Now the entire worth of a deed depends upon the motive, the intention. Doubtless objectives right & wrong exist but for each, individually, there exists only subjective right & wrong. An action intrinsically wrong would be right for me, if I fully believed it to be so, it could, in that case do me no moral harm. But the action done for the best objective end, (or with the apparently most excellent outward object in view) would deteriorate a character, if done from an unworthy motive. But further it is not always necessary to subjective rightness that it sh[oul]d be self conscious. An intrinsically wrong action, also subjectively wrong, (that is unredeemed by individual belief in its rightness) might yet be rendered harmless (i.e. justified) by the motive, self forgetfulness or sacrificing love of another, & this tho' the external object might be a wholly unworthy one.

Such independent thinking and questioning of her faith naturally led Lilian to reflect on her relationship with her mother, the most Victorian figure in her life, whose "fussiness, primness, and narrowness of mind drove most of her family to distraction" and "who took very little notice of her children when they were young" (Barker 22; Gindin, *John Galsworthy's Life and Art* 25-27). When she did take notice, Lilian and her sister Mabel "found her meticulousness almost unendurable," as she "was continually adjusting the set of the girls' dresses, or correcting some slightly slipshod expression they had uttered (Barker 23). Such treatment drove Lilian, when she was in her early twenties, to "wonder if it would lessen the accuteness [*sic*] of nervous irritation & asking which one incompatibility causes, to myself (& I imagine also to Mother) if I try to analyse it &, at any rate, put my feelings down!" In doing so, she wondered further

if it is purely physical the process that takes place in me at times set in action by her presence. I lie on this sofa thinking or reading, she comes in, says a word or 2 or perhaps not even that, cuts a pencil, walks about the room tidying up, looks at her plants, or even sits in her armchair reading & simply swings her foot; nothing more, even less, even her very presence, if the excitement has already been set up, is enough to produce this effect; a feeling of complete inability to fix my thoughts on this subject of study & horrible apprehension that the next moment will bring a remark, & that remark a small external criticism, sets up excitement of all my nerves, I shut my eyes, but I still see her, & I try to exclude the subtle influence which normally has no effect but the apparent tightening of my nerves resulting in positive pain, & soreness all over. I do not think I ever have experienced this in the same degree from contact with anyone else, but that is probably thro' my never having been thrown so much with another! (Cadbury Library, JG(II)/10/2/1)

Lilian examined her mother even more critically by juxtaposing the distinguishing features of their personalities:

The fault, if fault there be, is as much, I am convinced, on one side as the other, but I am inclined to think that it is a matter beyond our control. What I want to know is, is the incompatibility one of the physical Nature = temperament, or of ego. No doubt the action of Mother's influence reaches my ego thro' my phys[ical] organs, but does it irritate them, immediately, or only by a reflex process thro' the irritation of the ego itself? I am inclined to the latter view, because I find that our characters, (= I suppose ego) are quite dissimilar; & that the more sympathetic (and in some mental respect like my own) a character: is, the less of this outward irritation its contact causes me. Physically I should think we are similarly constituted, neither strong, both nervous, whether the different construction of our brains would account for it I don't know, but I think it must be the different construction of our egos. Our characters (each as a whole) afford a striking contrast, & it is interesting to me to study the parallel with the points of convergence & divergence the comparison is the clue to many assortments of character I come across, with their riddles of compatibility & antagonism (Cadbury Library, JG(II)/10/2/1).

Lilian continued:

The principal difference, the 'great gulf fixed' between us is this: Mother's mind is essentially the reverse. My mind is essentially introspective, contemplative. Her organs of sight & sound & touch & the corresponding mental faculties are extraordinarily quick; & her critical faculty strongly developed; this developed almost entirely with use upon outward objects. It is a perfectly consistent mind & this key: externality (not triviality) unlocks the whole. I say it is not a trivial mind, for it is serious with the religious & emotional if not intellectual depths; but yet in one sense, in the strict sense, it is so, for it is more commonly and completely occupied with trifles, more acutely [?] sensible of petty matters than is compatible with any greatness. A great mind, true, can take in small matters & will be conscientious in the despatch of them, but can never be absorbed or satisfied with them. By externality I mean accute [*sic*] observation of & concentration of mind upon outward things, not an absence of reflection. The external mind exercises itself most congenially with household matters, it excells [*sic*] in domestic duties of house-keeping, & dressmaking; the arrangement of rooms, dresses & dinners & the management of servants etc. take a surprising amount of mind, but of the external kind. (My kind won't do at all, however much there may be of it) The external mind in its religious phase is full of feeling warm impulse & promptings to duty, but all attach themselves to outward objects: the outward forms of religion are much to such a mind, the outward demonstrations of affection much, duties are clearly defined, strongly binding, not only upon itself but in its opinion upon others, its creed, too, after it has taken perhaps some little pains to get 'the right' one, is binding, becomes more or less a 'dogma'. The external mind is infinitely pained by untidiness & attaches the greatest importance I have noticed to the following details: threads & pins being left about, books, papers etc. not put away, mistakes in grammar, spelling, or etiquette, above all small points crooked, or wrong in personal appearance. Whenever you go near this mind you feel as if you were nearing a large microscope & life becomes immediately a burden to the unhappy being whose hair is not becomingly 'done' who has a pin or a stitch showing, or not, or, most hopeless of all, whose dress whobbles! So entirely exclusively & quickly does this mind seize these details that if you come to it with a face full of trouble (& a heart presumably to match below) or a manner full of interest, (with a question one might imagine of equal interest behind) you will be greeted (& perhaps chilled & placed a little further from the range of future sympathy who knows), by the remark, 'don't walk with your legs tied together! you turn your toes in & twist your legs together in the funniest way', or – 'you haven't pinned your dress straight, how many more times shall I have to tell you?' It grows on one I suppose this habit of outwardness, till the mind cannot take in anything but the outward defect, fails to see thro' manner into other minds, blunts in time, not only the feelings (or the expression of them) of others but maybe of its own – I go up to some one of this nature with an important question or remark; it is like facing a fusilade; the glare of the external eye is on my bonnet! & a myriad little thoughts are busy within upon the rearrangement of pattern

or bow. What a tremendous peak it's in – would that I would take it off & let it be just altered a little! O, never mind, if I like to go a perfect fright, & as I whisk out of the door in a hurry, 'come back one minute & let me put a pin in your dress it's all on one side, & look here at this great piece of ravelling - I never saw such an untidy child, why can't you look in the glass & keep your self nice and I – am the v. reverse of all this, no practical good at all – As unobservant as an old bat, & as lazy as any one can well be – A dreamer who occasionally thinks & acts seldom & with extreme difficulty. A kind of mind which can walk straight into a drawing room at a dinner party with goloshes on – in unconsciousness supreme, after the manner of Hegel who is said to have left his shoe in the mud & walked home without missing it – A link! – a mind which can forget anything in the world or out of it – Whose self opinion varies with its company, or whose rights are not 'in the middle' but as the [printer?] very well put it 'in a muddle' – Introspective (Cadbury Library, JG(II)/10/2/1).
Underscoring, Lilian's detailed observations about the differences between herself and her mother—and no less her loss of faith—she composed "Thoughts of a Cartesian Sceptic," wherein she asked:

When I have dared to question 'are things so?'
To look a dogma in the face & say
'Art thou, whom all men deem the truth, a lie?'
Then have I struck the first defiant blow
For mental freedom, & a little way
Around me cleared [?]. But by that blow am I
Dissevered from this faith I held so dear,
Dissevered, mind & mind from friend & kin
Free, but in awful solitude of doubt
To wrestle with my dim discernéd fear,
To still the warring elements within
To heal the broken harmonies without…
(Cadbury Library, JG(II)/10/2/1).

Such trajectories of critical thinking, combined with her emerging and interconnected identities as a wife, a mother, and a poet, reveal how and why Lilian increasingly embraced a life of the mind and adherence to independence and suffragism.

Georg Sauter

Following their residence in Kensington Palace Mansions, Lilian and her family moved again, to 8 Cambridge Gate adjacent to Regent's

Park, a large white mansion which her father had built along with several others in the same street (Gindin, *Life and Art* 25) [Figure 6]. Here she would fall in love and, after marriage, time abroad, and the birth of her son, she would return to settle briefly before moving with her family to Holland Park, Kensington.

Figure 6
Postcard depicting Cambridge Gate, Regents Park N.W., where Lilian and her family moved in the late 1880s, following their residence in Kensington Palace Mansions. Collection and courtesy of the author.

One day in 1890, Lilian's friend Frances Knight-Bruce visited 8 Cambridge Gate accompanied by a handsome twenty-four-year-old Bavarian painter named Georg Sauter (Reznick 11-15; Stalla 73-87) [Figure 7].[1] He had recently arrived in the city through the generosity of a patron of his promising artistic career begun at the Royal Academy and developed through work in various parts of Europe, including Holland, Belgium, France, and Italy.

[1] Mabel's recollections are an invaluable source for reconstructing the relationship between Georg and Lilian and their roles as parents to Rudolf. Evidently, these recollections were unknown to Galsworthy biographers Dudley Barker and James Gindin who offered a different account of how Lilian met Georg. Citing no sources, Barker suggested that it was Lilian who saw Georg painting in the National Gallery, "brought him home to Cambridge Gate" where Georg first "began on Mabel" who "fell in love with him," but then "things turned out even worse" when the family learned that he was not "in love with Mabel but with Lilian and she with him: (34-35). Citing a May 22, 1974 interview with Muriel Galsworthy (John Galsworthy's niece), Gindin offered that Lilian and Mabel together saw Georg painting in the National Gallery and invited him home where he "started with Mabel,: who rejected his marriage proposal. Georg then proposed to Lilian (Gindin, *Life and Art* 48-49, and *The English Climate* 10).

Figure 7
Georg Sauter, self-portrait, ca. 1890, oil on board, 35 x 25.5 cm, completed around
the time he and Lilian met and began their courtship.
Courtesy of Robert and Jane Oldmeadow.

Frances had seen Georg in the National Gallery sketching Titian's *Bacchus and Ariadne* and was "struck by the excellence of the copy he was making" (Reynolds 74). She "opened conversation with him" and "soon became strongly impressed by his talent" and his determination "to stand on his own two feet and half-starved perhaps, but wholly indomitable [in his] fight for recognition in London." Frances became interested to find him paid work, so she brought him to the Galsworthys' home, hoping that the elder Galsworthy might let him paint his portrait.

The household into which Georg entered was "very 'Victorian'" and likely had a "devastating effect…on his art-loving eyes and soul," beginning with "the vast conventional drawing-room [which] must have been a shock." Therein, he saw "carpet and curtains…of crimson velvet…Buhl cabinets, white marble, consol-tables, gilt-edged mirrors, Dresden china ornaments, a Collard grand piano and water-colours by popular Royal Academicians." At the same time, Georg likely made his hosts as "uncomfortable" as he felt in their orderly Victorian home, as he was

> …a somewhat uncouth figure…clad in unconventional garments, but the head was striking…with rather long dark-brown hair, strong Wagnerian profile and keen blue eyes. He

knew very little English as yet; but Lilian's German was fairly equal to the occasion, though the translation of a philosophical work by Teichmüller on which, I remember, she was working at the time, was not, perhaps, the most useful preparation for colloquial conversation in homely German tinged with strong Bavarian dialect (Reynolds 74).

Despite his appearance and background—or perhaps as a result of it—the Galsworthys became enthralled with his background, experience, and expertise:

He talked vigorously and picturesquely and some of his opinions gave us rough, if healthy shakings, He had, for instance, a lively contempt for what he called the [informal chocolate-box] portraits in the Royal Academy; and doubtless found equally contemptible our comparative ignorance concerning such gods as Rembrandt, Whistler and Matthieu Maris. He waxed enthusiastic over Lenbach of Munich, in whose studio/workspace he had received kindness and helpful advice and he talked about many another painter, both 'ancient and modern', of whom we had never heard. His eyes constantly strayed in my Father's direction and once or twice, in complete oblivion of surroundings and company, he would shoot out a broad hand—considerably constrained by paint and cigarettes—and caress the air, with a curious, semi-circular, sweeping movement. He was composing the possible future picture in his mind's eye! (Reynolds 75).

Embraced by the family for his obvious skill and "infectious enthusiasm," Georg eventually embarked on his portrait of the elder Galsworthy, visiting the home on multiple occasions and transforming its drawing room into his studio. With each visit, Lilian not only observed his painting take shape but also Georg himself as he worked. "In the bay window sat my sister always," Mabel recalled, "her translation or other work on a table in front of her—artist and canvas well within her view." She observed Georg with her "eager shining eyes" which "seemed to drink in his excitedly-expressed ideas humbly, thirstily, without reservation" because

to watch him paint was a revelation. He worked with feverish intensity. Darting at the canvas as though he wanted to annihilate it, he would lay the paint on with a kind of fierce tenderness, impossible to describe. Then, springing back, he would survey the picture from a distance, his eyes ablaze and his broad hand— in which the slender brush looked as much out of place as a pin in the jaws of a steam-hammer—waving wildly, or stroking the air with the 'composing gesture', before violently attacking tubes and pallette again with a view to some fresh and subtle combination of colour (Reynolds 76).

Beyond falling in love as she observed Georg and he inspired her intellectual pursuits, Lilian continued to navigate her own intellectual interests despite lingering Victorian separate spheres. Expected by her parents—and wider society—to remain and grow in her domestic role, self-sacrificing and managing the household, she desired otherwise to live and grow in the public domain and participate in its prevailing ethic of work and achievement.

As Georg conveyed his inspiration, passion, and enthusiasm for the arts, he tapped into creative interests which Lilian held dear. Mabel later explained the situation for her sister being that

a new door to spiritual freedom was rapidly opening—new aspects were swiftly presenting themselves of existence and of art. The very crudity and violence of his feelings and expressions were an attraction; their independence [sic] fascinated her diffident nature and drew her wonder and covert applause. To both of us, indeed, it was an exciting upheaval—the sudden encounter with his volcanic nature, with its combination of the elemental (Ursprünglichkeit) and the artistic (Künstlerschaft), its almost fanatical urge for work and its detestation of 'Pfuscherei' [bad-job] of any kind" (Reynolds 76).

Perhaps inspired by Georg's "volcanic nature," yet certainly by their love for each other, Lilian composed the following untitled poem for him during the Christmas season of 1890:

O speak! We are alone!
  Breathe once the word divine,
  Soft! The fire flickers on the wall.
  Round thy dear form the shadows fall
  Thy hand is pressed in mine,
  Thy soul and mine are one.

Breathe soft the word, & low,
  The word I scarce dare name
  Lest the rude world should, waking
                hear
  Let the world sleep, too rude its ear
  For aught my lips would frame
  For aught thy heart should know.

Breathe "Friendship", word of mine
  For all the heart holds dear
  Love that the purest soul can feel
  Trust, or support, in woe or weal,

Aye all that draws thee near,
And links my soul with thine.

Aye, strength to fight, & strive,
  By loss, & labour gain,
  Love that will wait, & trust, & pray,
  Love that can give without repay,
  Can give, & take but pain,
  Can suffer, die, or live.

O take the word, t'is mine,
  With all its power to bless,
  "Friendship", what more can this life bring?
  What fuller, what diviner thing,
  Can thy dear life express?
  T'is love, but love divine.

Following their courtship of several years, their engagement in 1892, and Lilian's parents ultimately respecting their love, Lilian and Georg married on July 17, 1894. Their marriage ceremony took place in St. Mary Magdalene Church, Munster Square, London. Lilian wore "a pearl heart" and carried "a bouquet of her name-flower, lilies," both gifts from Georg ("Approaching Marriages," "The Weddings of the Week"). Shortly thereafter, they travelled to Bavaria. Their destination was the Kneipp health resort in Wörishofen, the center of the Natural Cure Movement of Germany, a form of hydrotherapy practiced by Father Sebastian Kneipp. Here Lilian hoped to find comfort and relief from her frail health, and Georg hoped to find artistic inspiration. As they found what they were seeking, they became parents, on May 9, 1895, when Lilian gave birth to a boy, Rudolf Helmut. The family remained in Wörishofen through most of the following year before spending time in Italy where Lilian composed "Painting in Venice," a loving acrostic poem about Georg and his artistic talent:

Gazing o'er the changing water
Eagle – with those hands for wings,
Out of Fate's haphazard beauties
Radiant loveliness he brings.
Genius lights his marvellous vision
Shapes his brush's faintest line,
Azure depths and whitest towers
Under his creating shrine.
Thrilling on the magic canvas
Everlasting beauty caught,
Renaissance of spirit taught.

Motherhood and Health

In the spring of 1897, the family returned to London, settling in 8 Cambridge Gate where she and Georg had met and fallen in love (Reynolds 83). As Lilian increasingly found her voice as a poet, she became a loving mother, spending quality time with Rudolf, together reading, sketching, exploring nature, and sharing artistic and literary creations. Georg captured their closeness in his painting *Maternity* [Figure 8]. When Rudolf entered Harrow in 1909, Lilian remained in close touch, visiting him frequently, lifting his spirits when his schoolwork and social situations became stressful, and celebrating with him on occasions of his academic success (Reznick 34-35). After the war, when Rudolf married Viola Ada Emily Wood, Lilian embraced her as warmly as him, as she wrote to her friend Ethel Fiedler in late December 1922:

Figure 8

Maternity by Georg Sauter, ca. 1899, oil on canvas, 69.9 x 49.5 cm.
Courtesy of and ©Research and Cultural Collections, University of Birmingham.

My boy as perhaps you know is married!—to the dear girl who lived with us, & was more than a daughter to me during the war. She had been married before but very unhappily & had left her husband already when she came to stay with us. We have known her for many years & she is as good as she is beautiful. Rudo & she were deeply devoted to each other & as soon as she obtained her freedom they were married & are supremely happy It is my greatest comfort that we can all live happily together (Lilian to Ethel Fiedler, Taylor Institution Library, MS.G/Sauter L.1).

They did live happily together, in Freeland, Holders Hill, London, where Lilian eventually composed her loving tribute "To Viola":

You came to us in days of lonely
 grief
When loss was new, a bitter cup to drain
And life was full of problems and relief
Seemed far from all the
 weariness and strain,
You came with Love, Love
 let you in with joy.
Love held the key that made
 our three lives one
Made you to me a daughter,
 to my boy
The Love, the life, the joy the
 very sun.
O faithful soul whose every
 thought is strong
To duty's pitch, whose days
 are one long round
Of Loving service, yet whose
 joy is hung
On all delight and beauty
 you had found
You Love the spring of Life
 the joy, the way
May Love be with you
 through and endless day.

The first decade of the new century also saw Lilian continue to struggle with ill health and how best to manage it in her busy life with Rudolf, Georg, and an increasingly productive and growing reputation as a poet. In early May 1910, her mother was planning a trip to Bagnoles de l'Orne in Normandy, to "take the baths" there for her symptoms of rheumatism, and she encouraged Lilian to come along. "I dare say they would be good," Lilian wrote to Georg with some hesitation, "but I do *not want* to go. Of course if you were going to be away I would go – or if Mother would go *now*. But she thinks it too cold still and too hot in July. Do write by return & tell me what you think about my going at all. I will *not* go with her in the *holidays*....My Gele, I kiss you a thousand thousand times" (Lilian to Georg, Cadbury Library, JG(II)/9/1). Such love and companionship became hallmarks of the life Lilian and Georg built together with Rudolf in their next home.

Lilian's Circle in and beyond Holland Park, London

Shortly after Lilian, Georg, and Rudolf had returned from Wörishofen to London, they moved to 1 Holland Park Avenue, Kensington, through the generosity of Lilian's father who had bought the lease to the property.[2] In this neighbourhood of notables, Lilian and her family eventually became notables themselves in a milieu of artistry, activism, and sociability. This culture would infuse their lives for eighteen years before the Great War would change everything (Reznick 21-31).

Taking its name from the nearby grounds of the Jacobean mansion called Holland House, Holland Park was an idyllic hub of upper-middle-class Edwardian sociability. It encompassed the impressive Phillimore Estate and the ornate, well-to-do areas of Campden Hill Square and The Royal Crescent designed by the planner Robert Cantweld. During the late 19th century, a number of notable artists and art collectors lived in the area, most notably "The Holland Park Circle" of artists including Lord Leighton Frederic, Valentine Prinsep, and George Fredric Watts, among others. By Lilian's day, Holland Park had become home to many distinguished educational leaders, businessmen, religious leaders and physicians and surgeons (*Royal Blue Book* 320). Down the street and above the poulterer's and fishmonger's shops of 84 Holland Park Avenue was the home of Ford Madox Hueffer (later Ford), editor of *The English Review*, the major literary journal of the day in which Lilian would later publish her poetry. Like the Sauters, Ford frequently hosted "congenial parties that brought literary people together" (Ruedy 44; 87). Other prominent neighbours included Thomas Dutton, the physician and author; Joseph Lichtenfeld, London's leading wig-maker; Ernestine Evans Mills (née Bell) the artist, writer, and suffragette; John Sollie Henry, the cabinetmaker, and Ada S. Ballin, the well-known

---

[2] Lilian and Georg also settled in 1 Holland Park thanks to sister Mabel who, with her new husband, Thomas Reynolds, had noticed the property during the course of their own house-hunting. Mabel and Thomas settled into 10 Tor Gardens, Campden Hill, near to brother John who lived in 16a Aubrey Walk. See Barker 53.

author, editor and magazine proprietor of children's and women's magazines (UC Davis; Gomersall; Reznick 18). Comfortably situated and following in the footsteps of The Holland Park Circle, Lilian and Georg established their own circle in 1 Holland Park, which had its own prominent history. London developer James Brace had built it during the early 1820, and it was augmented with a studio in the 1860s around the time when Alexander Constantine Ionides, the prominent shipping owner and art collector, purchased it for himself and his family. William Holman Hunt, the pre-Raphaelite painter and one of the founders of the Pre-Raphaelite Brotherhood, had occupied the residence before the Sauters made it their own.

Boosting the prestige of 1 Holland Park was the loving investment of Lilian's father in converting its top floor into a large studio naturally lit by twenty-foot-high windows on the North and South sides. According to Ralph Hale Mottram, a close friend of the family, this impressive space had

> all the impedimenta—easels, curtains, frames and paints, pushed against the walls or stacked in a gallery to make room, in a more domestic and "homey" atmosphere than is perhaps common in such places, for a large and well-stocked tea-table, the cups, plates and hot-water dish upon which were dominated by a Russian samovar, covered by a special straw-woven cosy (Mottram 28).

The setting, Mottram described further, was

> presided over by Mrs. Lilian Sauter, who won my rather overawed provincial heart with the first glance of her beautiful grey-blue eyes. Smaller-boned and more obviously hypersensitive than her brother, either from the strain of being a painter's wife, or uneasily accepted maternity, or merely the new awareness of social injustice around, she was already slightly grey and worn. Or it may have been from the extra effort she put into the delicate verses she somehow contrived to write amid her other preoccupations. Beautifully dressed, with just a touch to show her devotion to the arts and to the current internationalism that differentiated her from the average Kensington hostess, she made me welcome (Mottram 28-29).

In fact, as suggested in a letter Lilian wrote to Georg in October 1910, she had a direct hand in crafting the decor of her home, a role she embraced in her particular way, as a partner with her husband, and perhaps while navigating recollections of her mother's extreme view of housekeeping rooted firmly in Victorian separate sphere ideology and practice (Lilian to Georg, Cadbury Library, JG(II)/9/1). Such attention contributed to the very "framework" of this home, as Mottram saw it, "the house itself, the money that kept it going, the lightly-held social rules that governed it, were utterly English," even while "much of the furniture, many of the sentiments, were derived thankfully from anywhere beyond these islands" (Mottram 29). Herbert Furst of *The Art Record* echoed Mottram's perspective on the residence, observing it to be exquisitely representative of Georg's artistic identity and rising international reputation:

> No sooner have you entered Sauter's house than a mysterious atmosphere surrounds you—a peaceful harmonious feeling and though you may not have seen the man yet—you feel his presence. His staircase is white and the carpets dark green. The walls are hung with reproductions from the artist's paintings and his invisible presence greets you: Welcome in *my* house. His studio is large and not crowded—in fact, you are able to see everything that is in it and everything has its reason to be where it is; the easels, the chairs, the crowded writing-table; the huge red brick fireplace and the large old-fashioned bellows, everything seems conscious of its duty which consists in making a *milieu* for the man to whom they belong. All this, though you may not think so, is very important and concerns Sauter the man more than you probably admit…You enter his studio and if you are possessed of the gift of looking into and not at things you know at once that you have entered the domains of a real artist… Sauter's house is very quiet—full of harmony—the noise has been transformed into a silent music and the theme is *adagio consolante* (Furst 665).

Inspired by this peaceful and creative milieu, Lilian composed "May Night," wherein she described her home as a "heart of peace." In so doing, she entered into dialog with Georg's contemporary painting of Holland Park, *Spring Night in London* [Figure 9], each supporting the other in observing and appreciating their domestic and urban surrounds:

Come out from the rush and the turmoil,
Out of the flaring street
Home to the hush of the garden,
Shadowy, silent, sweet.

Steal through the quivering darkness
Under the wings of night,
Feel the caress of the shadows
Chasing the silver light.

Scents of lilac and hawthorn
Hang in the limpid air;
Tenderly things are unfolding,
Blossoming everywhere.

Low in the intricate borders
Lily and Lupin bloom,
Lifting their tremulous fingers
Up through the twilit gloom.

Over the slumbering houses
Luminous, pale and high,
Trembling meshes of silver
Veil the deepening sky.

Tender, covering darkness
Bringer of pain's release,
Gather your querulous children
Close to the heart of peace.

Quelling the clamour of colour,
Stilling the strident hue,
Making a mystical music
Under the dome of blue.

Chords of darkening splendour,
Clash of immerging glow,
Tremours, where palpable, tender
Rhythmical shadows flow.

Hold us with passionate seeing,
Stirring those secret strings,
Dumb in the depths of our being,
Down at life's silent springs.

Self in us, deeper than thought, swings
Swayed in the trance of life,
Touching the essence of all things,
Under the sleeping strife.

Breathes in the intimate stillness.
Flower-like unfolds to the light,
Sings: "We are one, one with the whole
In the infinite song of the night."

Figure 9
Spring Night in London by George Sauter, ca. 1908, oil on canvas, 60.9 x 81.3 cm.
Courtesy of Leeds Art Gallery.

Beyond being a familial "heart of peace," 1 Holland Park became a focal point of sociobility through "fourth-Sunday at-home" salons which Lilian and Georg hosted for a wide range of guests. These individuals included Georg's associate James McNeill Whistler, who, Rudolf later recalled in his biography of his uncle, "was very fond of my mother," as well as John Macallan Swan, the award-winning English painter and sculptor, and Prince Pierre Troubetskoy, humanitarian and best man at Lilian and Georg's wedding. Many other notables also participated: Richard Aldington, Laurence Binyon, Joseph Conrad, Campell Dodgson, James Gutherie, Hubert Herkomer, Ezra Pound, Joseph Pennell, G.F. Watts, and even Mark Twain, who, Rudolf also recalled, "discussed philosophy, religion and Survival [sic] with my mother" (Gindin, *Life and Art* 49; Rudolf Sauter 35).

Observations of the Natural World

The natural world beyond her treasured home became a frontier Lilian explored with inquisitiveness, enthusiasm, and artistic talent, as her sketchbooks reveal. Herein with a pencil and much patience, and likely inspired by reading Darwin's *Origin of Species*, she sketched a sea of life: tadpoles "with hind legs just developing," baby newts, water beetles and water scorpions and their larvae, gnats and their pupae, water spiders and their eggs, a "jelly like creature almost invisible to the naked eye," and the "head of a small wriggling worm" [Figure 10].

She also sketched myrtle and leaves being eaten by beetle, the latter enhanced with watercolours, as well as several buildings located the rural areas she visited during this period.

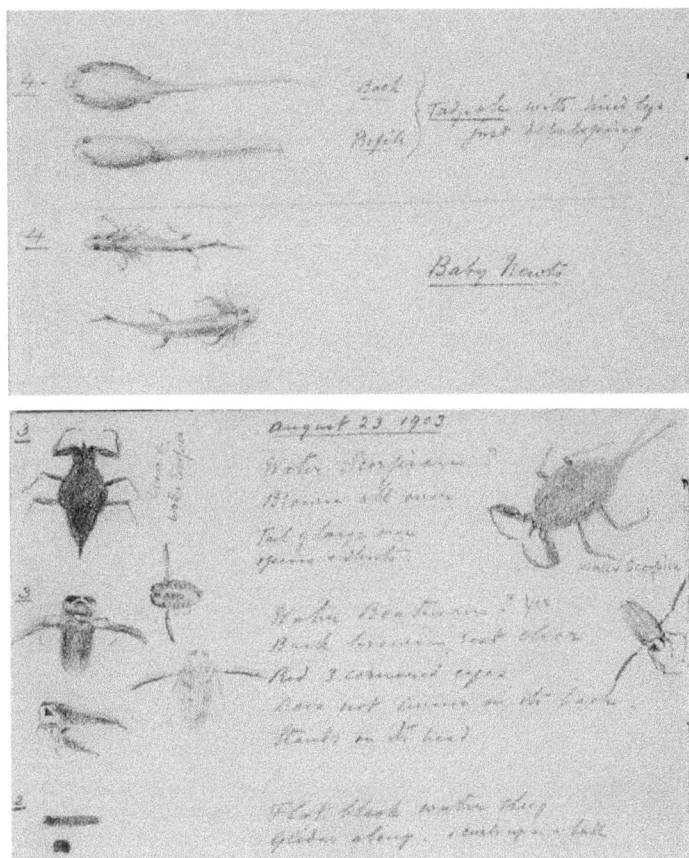

Figure 10
Selected sketchbook drawings and notes by Lilian Sauter, ca. 1903-5.
Courtesy of University of Birmingham, Cadbury Library, JG(II)/10/4.

Travel, Literary Productivity, and Achievement

Life further beyond Holland Park, across England and overseas, provided additional inspiration to Lilian as she pursued her writing. Her diary of 1907 documents a "heavenly day" on March 31 when she "made [a] poem," namely "Easter Morning," and another, on April 6, when she composed "London Spring," which celebrated the arrival of the season with blooming flowers and golden light (Cadbury Library, JG(II)/10/1). Lilian would select these pieces for inclusion in *Through*

High Windows. Notably, they brought to life Georg's contemporary work, *Spring Mood 1908*, again suggesting an intimate creative dialogue that was a cornerstone of their partnership [Figure 11].

Around this period, Lilian also composed "Streets of Gold," which contrasted the allure of London's vibrant streets with the struggles and suffering of its inhabitants, as well as "Sovereignty," which reflected on the symbolism of an unnamed arch and the individual's sovereignty in the face of mortality. She would also select these poems to appear in *Through High Windows*, immediately following her poems that were in dialogue with Georg, "London Spring" and "Easter Morning."

Figure 11
Spring Mood by Georg Sauter, 1908, oil on canvas, 112.4 x 92.7 cm.
Courtesy of Leeds Art Gallery.

During summer of 1908, Lilian and her family travelled to Cornwall [Figure 12]. There, she found inspiration to compose "Trevone. Song I: Minor Key" and "Trevone. Song II: Major Key," depicting her observations of grey hills and rocks, purple pools, and the motion of the sea (Cadbury Library, JG(II)/10/1). Lilian would select the former to open *Through High Windows*, following it with the latter.

Figure 12
Postcard depicting Trevone, near Padstow, Cornwall, England, ca. 1890-1900, where Lilian travelled during the summer of 1908, inspiring her compose "Trevone. Song I: Minor Key" and "Trevone. Song II: Major Key. Courtesy of the Library of Congress.

In August and September 1909, Lilian and her family travelled to Lucerne, Lauterbrunnen, and Schynige Platte, Switzerland, where scenery inspired her to compose several poems that would also appear in *Through High Windows* [Figure 13]. These works included "Eternal

Figure 13
Postcard depicting Schynige Platte, Switzerland, ca. 1890-1900, where Lilian travelled during the late summer and early fall of 1909, and inspired her to compose "The Earth Speaks," "Astrantia," "Storm Cry," "Still Life," and "Eternal Snows." Courtesy of the Library of Congress.

Snows" and "Schynige Platte," as well as "Astrantia," describing the pale ashen flower of the region which symbolized strength and bravery. She also composed "Still Life," depicting a serene and rocky valley framing gentle movements of a stream, "Storm Cry" after witnessing "thunderstorms [of] glorious wild effect," and "The Earth Speaks," which invited the reader to find rest and solace in the embrace of nature. Additionally during this period, she wrote "a sonnet on Georg," a piece which would appear in *Through High Windows* as "To G.S.," praising his candour and strength and comparing him to the elements of nature (Cadbury Library, JG(II)/10/1).

Following their time in Switzerland, the family visited Bavaria, Germany, where they spent time with Georg's father and took in an exhibition of "Rheinisch Artists." They travelled next to Frankfurt and the first German International Aviation Exhibition [Figure 14]. There, Lilian witnessed a "Zeppelin III flying, & the Hall full of aeroplane models," a "Parsival fly," and a German-built version of the Wright Brothers' flying machine on display (Cadbury Library, JG(II)/10/1). This experience, perhaps combined with reading contemporary newspaper accounts of early flights, likely inspired her to compose "The Aviator" wherein she explored the exhilaration and freedom of flying and contemplated the potential of human progress. This piece, along with others of this travel period, would join her selected others in *Through High Windows*.

Figure 14
Postcard depicting the International Airship Exhibition, Frankfurt, 1909, which Lilian visited during her travels and likely inspired her to compose "The Aviator."
Courtesy of Wellcome Collection.

Publishing success followed Lilian's several years of writing and traveling. In its July 1910 review of magazines, *The Common Cause* pointed out to its readers that in the new issue of *The Englishwoman* "there is a beautiful sonnet by Lilian Sauter" ("The Magazines"). Such was the reception of what was her first published work, namely "Storm-Cry." In just over a year, this piece joined five others in the pages of *The Englishwoman*: "Astrantia," "Trevone," "To Love," "Still Life," and "Woman." The editors of *The Woman Worker* took notice and featured "Astrantia" in their March 1910 highlights of "Women in the Press." Lilian would select all of these poems for inclusion in *Through High Windows*.

In September 1910, Lilian achieved further publishing success when her fellow Holland Park neighbor Ford Madox Hueffer featured two of her poems, "The Aviator" and "The Pause," in his prestigious *English Review*, alongside the work of many respected contemporaries (Reznick 25-27) [Figure 15].

```
The English Review

Contributors for September
Frank Harris            H. G. Wells
Hilaire Belloc          Vernon Lee
R. A. Scott James       Hugh Walpole
William Beckford        W. S. Blunt
T. E. Green             James Stephens
C. N. Robinson          Lilian Sauter

Professor Otto Most
"The Problem of Unemployment in Germany."

All communications respecting " The English Review " to be
addressed to The Manager, 11, Henrietta St., London, W.C.
```

Figure 15
Advertisement for the September 1910 issue of *The English Review* from *The Studio: An Illustrated Magazine of Fine and Applied Art* 50, no. 210, September 15, 1910, p. 210. Courtesy of Google via Google Books.

Declaring "The Aviator" to be "a quite notable effort," *The Globe* quoted one of its verses:
For once to measure with an infinite span
The little things of earth, from heaven's great height,

And thence to view the works and ways of man,
And judge their values with a clearer sight!

O Joy! to race the winds, and hear them singing,
To cleave the clouds, and spring, and swoop, and rise,
And on and on, in the infinite, up-winging,
With throbbing pulse, and sun-confronting eyes!
The editors of *The Living Age* also noted the appearance of "The Aviator" in *The English Review*, and they reprinted it in their magazine alongside works by William Watson and Guy Kendall. The editors of *The Argonaut* did the same, placing it with current verse by Arthur Chapman, William Watson, Berton Braley, and Richard Wightman. The poem even appeared in *The Province* newspaper of Vancouver, British Columbia, and in the *Jackson Daily News* of Jackson, Mississippi, thus extending her audience overseas.

During this period, *The Vineyard* featured Lilian's poem "Poet's Work," which seemed to encapsulate her lifelong literary dreams:
To pluck a thought out from the heart of life,
Plunge it in molten words and fling it high!
A flaming banner in the gloom of strife,
A beacon blazing in a storm-swept sky...
Soon after the appearance of this piece, which Lilian would also select for inclusion in *Through High Windows*, the Women's Printing Society published her "Women's Highest Plea for Suffrage." This achievement marked another significant chapter of her life, reflecting her political activism and affiliations (Reznick 28-29).

Humanism and Suffragism

During Lilian's residence in Holland Park, travels in Europe, and productivity in writing, she held memberships in the West London Ethical Society and the London Society for Women's Suffrage (*Annual Reports of the West London Ethical Society, 1898-1901*). Likely through one or both of these associations, or perhaps through one of her "fourth-Sunday at-home" salons, she connected with the Women Writers' Suffrage League (WWSL), an organization established in 1908 by Cicely Hamilton and Bessie Hatton to "obtain the vote for women on the same terms as it is or may be granted to men" through "methods proper to writers—the use of the pen" [Figure 16] (A.J.R. 137). Through this mission, the WWSL supported the publications of many authors, including *How the Vote Was Won: A Play in One Act* (1909) by Hamilton and C. Hedley Charlton; *The Suffrage Question*

(1909) by Madeleine Lucette Ryley; *A Pageant of Great Omen* (1909) also by Hamilton; "Women's Cause" (1909), a poem by Laurence Housman; *Why* (1910) and *Under His Roof* (1912) by Elizabeth Robins; *Lady Geraldine's Speech* (1910) by Beatrice Harraden; *Feminism* (1912) by May Sinclair, and a cartoon postcard of "Justice" by W. H. Margetson (Robins 225-226). Lilian's own suffragist work would soon join this distinguished canon.

Figure 16
Postcard produced by the Women Writers' Suffrage League, 1909, depicting a woman appealing to Justice for protection from "Prejudice" as a man pulls her back by her sash. Courtesy of The New York Public Library.

Lilian's organizational affiliations extended beyond the West London Ethical Society, London Society for Women's Suffrage, and WWSL. She supported the International Women's Relief Committee by donating funds, interviewing applicants for relief, and investigating their difficulties ("The International Women's Relief Committee – I"), and International Women's Suffrage Association ("Honorary Associates' Subscriptions"). Moreover, she served first as temporary honorary secretary of the Spiritual Militancy League for the Women's Charter of Rights and Liberties, and then formally as its secretary ("Spiritual Militancy League for the Women's Charter of Rights and Liberties)." Women's Freedom League member Adela Coit had established the league in 1913 "with the object of showing in a militant manner without violence that Woman Suffrage has a spiritual connection and is not a purely secular movement" ("Militancy for Non-Militants," "A New League). As its manifesto stated:

> We have banded ourselves together with the aim of concentrating attention upon the spiritual and vital issues involved in the women's movement. We desire to unite all who believe that the supreme power of woman is spiritual power, and from this point of view we would make a greater effort than has yet been made to awaken the imagination and rouse the conscience of the public as to the wrongs suffered by women, and through them by the community. We intend to resort to no methods of violence nor any action which may endanger life or property, but by concentration upon the ideal of social justice, by reliance upon the spiritual force which is at the heart of all progress, by perfectly peaceful protest, by extending the knowledge of the women's charter, and by working for the reforms it advocates we will attempt to create an irresistible wave of public opinion in favour of the complete emancipation of women ("Orange and Black").

One of the chief aims of the league, was to "attend church services" toward "evoking...spiritual force to advance social justice for women, and the linking up of the women's causes with religion and the Churches." Paving the way to this intention, the league sent a letter "to the clergy of the Established Church and similar letters to the preachers of the various Free Churches." Signed by Adela Coit and endorsed by Lilian, and by Lady Aberconway, Adeline Chapman, Charlotte Despard, Olive Mackirdy, Margaret McMillan, and Flora Steel," the letter stated:

> We are confident that it would be of untold advantage to the nation if you would instruct and inspire, on this great issue of the day, the men and women who look to your pulpit for

guidance. And, even if you decide against us, we would ask you to make your reasons known, so that the public may benefit by your judgement...We feel that there is little hope of securing the vote for women or preparing them for a moral and spiritual use of it so long as the 50,000 preachers throughout the nation by silence and neutrality create the impression that none of the higher issues of life are involved in the suffrage movement ("Orange and Black").

Despite the pledge of the Spiritual Militancy League to "no methods of violence nor any action which may endanger life or property," newspapers reporting on the February 1913 arson attack on the Tea Pavilion in Kew Gardens associated the organization with the broader militant suffragist movement. Herein they also explicitly named Lilian as the League's "temporary honorary secretary" ("Suffragists Burn a Pavilion at Kew").[3] Lilian's diary contains no indication that she was present at Kew Gardens on that day, or that she participated in the attack (Cadbury Library, JG(II)/10/1).[4]

Through High Windows...and More

On June 2, 1911, the London Society for Women's Suffrage convened a "Meeting for Working Women" in Queen's Hall, Langham Place. The program included "a new song to be performed by Margaret Layton," namely Lilian's "Women's Song of Freedom," which Annette Hullah, the noted musician and biographer of Theodor Leschetizky, had set to music.[5] A few months later, on November 2, Auriol Lee, the popular British stage actress, recited Lilian's "Woman's Plea" as part of a widely publicized public meeting of the WWSL in the Great Hall of the Criterion in Piccadilly Circus ("The Women Writers' Suffrage League") [Figures 17-19]. These performances point to the acceptance of Lilian's work, if not its outright popularity in contemporary suffragist circles, as does the contemporary initiative of the Women's Printing Society publishing "Woman's Highest Plea for Suffrage"

[3] See also "Militancy for Non-Militants," "Suffragette Incendiaries," "Fire Outrage at Kew Gardens," and :A New League." All of these articles identified Lilian as "temporary honorary secretary" of the Spiritual Militancy League.

[4] In fact, her diary entries during the week of the attack appear to be early drafts of the poetry about her friend Frieda and daughter-in-law Viola, discussed below.

[5] Nelson includes Lilian's "Women's Song of Freedom" in her seminal collection of women's suffrage literature but without the music composed by Hullah (173). I hope that the convergence of the text and music here inspires a new production of the work, which would likely be the first since its original production in 1911.

through an agreement between Lilian and WWSL (Cadbury Library, JG(II)/10/3). Notably, the first page of this leaflet featured the same etching of lilies, Lilian's namesake flower, which had appeared on the first page of *Through High Windows*, wherein Lilian paired "Woman's Plea for Suffrage" and "Woman's Song of Freedom" to conclude the volume.[6]

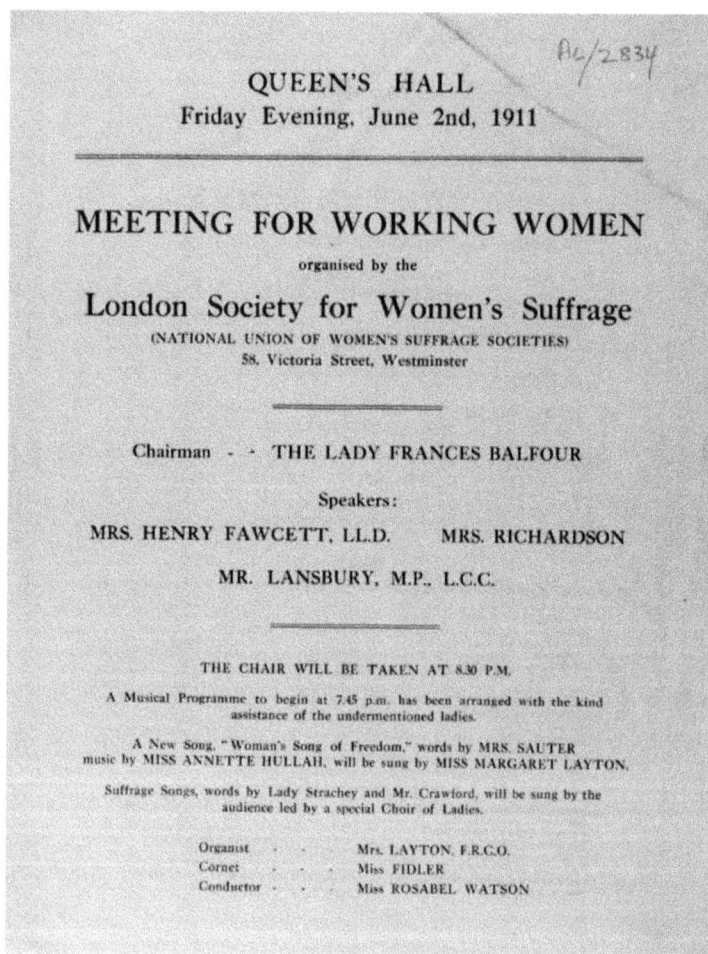

Figure 17

Meeting program of the London Society for Women's Suffrage, June 2, 1911. Courtesy of the LSE Digital Library.

---

[6] It is unknown why Lilian removed "Highest" in the title of the version which appeared in *Through High Windows*. Apart from this difference, the poems are identical.

Figure 18
"Woman's Song of Freedom," leaflet. Courtesy of the British Library.

Figure 19
Left: Photograph of Annette Hullah, ca. 1900, the noted musician and biographer of
Theodor Leschetizky, who set to music Lilian's poem "Women's Song of Freedom."
Courtesy of The Bancroft Library.

Right: Photograph of Auriol Lee, 1910s, bromide press print, the popular British
stage actress who recited Lilian's "Woman's Plea" during a widely publicized fall 1911
meeting of the Women Writers' suffrage League.
Courtesy of the National Portrait Gallery.

Through High Windows was as much a product of Lilian's life in and
beyond Holland Park as it was a culmination of her longstanding interest
in conveying the beauty of the natural world. With the cover price of
1 shilling and 6 pence, the book appeared in 1911 from the publisher
Curtis and Davison, the namesake of Lilian's fellow Kensington
residents Adela Marion Curtis (1867-1960) and Lily Davison Cancellor
(1864-1928) [Figure 20].[7] It was printed by the Chiswick Press, a
pioneer of the production of quality books at reasonable prices and
smaller-sized books—like *Through High Windows*—which were easy to
fit into a pocket ("Chiswick Press and The Chiswick Shakespeare").
    Located in 11a Church Street, Kensington, Curtis and Davison
was a progressive business which encompassed a new and second-
hand bookstore as well as a bookbinder and circulating library (Curtis
and Davison to Edward Gordon Craig, 16 October 1912, Ransom

[7] Indeed, all three women likely lived near each other, and perhaps, through her
faith and spiritual writings, Curtis associated herself, like Lilian, with the Spiritual
Militancy League. Thanks very much Elizabeth Goodacre and Madeleine Goodall,
Humanists UK, for suggesting these connections.

Center). It likely sold *Through High Windows* in its own store along with other books it had published, including *A Third Pot-Pourri* (1903) by Maria Theresa Earle, the British horticulturist, writer on garden subjects, and friend of Adela Curtis; Curtis's own book, *The New Mysticism: Six Lectures Given in Kensington, and at Cobham, Surrey* (1906), and Marion F. Smithes' *Children of the Desert* (1910) with photographs by W.H. Edgar. Stock of Curtis and Davison bookshop also included such "useful pamphlets" as *Forty Vegetarian Dinners*; *Science in the Daily Meal*; *Fruits, Nuts and Vegetables: Their Uses as Food and Medicine*; *A New Era for Women: Health without Drugs*, and *The Perfect Way in Diet* (Earle 26-29). At least one more title would follow from the press, namely James Rhoades' *Wedding Rhymes* (ca. 1912). Subsequently, the name of the press changed to The Settlement Press, which published Curtis's own *Sex and Money: By the Warden of the Household of Silence* (ca. 1934).

Figure 20
Left: Cabinet card depicting Adela Marion Curtis (detail), ca. mid 1880s.
Right: Photograph of Lily Davison Cancellor, date unknown.
Courtesy of Jeremy Jay and The Othona Community.

As mentioned at the beginning of this introduction, when *Through High Windows* appeared *The Poetry Review* called it "a little book worth reading," explaining that "Mrs. Sauter's verse reaches a fairly high level of attainment. Such poems as 'Trevone,' 'Storm Cry,' 'Eternal Snows,' reflecting on majestic peaks, the journey of life, and seeking of peace and transcendence, display a remarkable insight into Nature's spiritual significance, and strong descriptive powers" (*"Through High Windows"* 234). A writer in *The Guardian* offered a slightly tempered but nonetheless positive review:

xlvii

Mrs. Lilian Sauter has concentrated a great deal of vigorous and vivid feeling into a small collection of verses…The half-dozen sonnets are a rather weak spot in the volume and Mrs. Sauter's energetic plea for the suffrage, an excellent plea, is, as a poem, too explanatory. She suffers from a tendency to allow poetic seriousness to overheat itself as it takes form; yet several of her shorter lyrics—and we should like to mention in particular that called 'To Love'—burn with a clear heat of which no part is wasted ("Recent Verse").

Following the publication of *Through High Windows*, Lilian's poem "The Pause" appeared in the June 1914 issues of *The Englishwoman*, associated with the National Union of Women's Suffrage Societies, and *Jus Suffragii*, the official journal of International Woman Suffrage Alliance. She continued to write, but the advent of the Great War would profoundly disrupt her life. Only one more of her poems from *Through High Windows*, namely "Heart-Lighted," would appear in print. Ursula Greville, the British soprano and editor of *The Sackbut* included the piece in her May 1924 issue alongside works by several eminent music critics, including Robin H. Legge, A. Walter Kramer, Jerome Hart, F.H. Martens, and John F. Porte.

The Great War

On August 5, 1914, one day after England declared war on Germany, Parliament passed the Aliens Restriction Act, requiring foreign nationals, particularly Germans, to register with the police and, when necessary, be interned or deported (Reznick 41-42; Stibbe 91-93). As Georg described the situation to his friend Ethel Fiedler, "[t]he calamity which has come over us is so terrible and paralysing, we [are] dumb." (Georg Sauter to Ethel Fiedler, September 3, 1914, Taylor Institution Library). Despite this climate of widespread anti-German sentiment and fear of spies, Georg and Lilian sought to live as usual. He continued to paint. She continued to write and expand her involvement in suffragist circles. Rudolf continued the studies he had begun in Munich a few years earlier, and he spent time at Wingstone, his uncle's farmhouse in Manaton, Devon, riding horses and walking in the countryside (Marrot 413). The normalcy all three Sauters attempted to achieve belied the fact that "the shadow of war was creeping closer to them" (Mottram 184).

Indeed, the rule of wartime law eventually caught up with the family when authorities interned Georg on December 7, 1915 (Georg Sauter to Harrison Morris, December 9, 1919, Princeton University

Library). The action appalled his family and friends, and especially Lilian's brother John, who soon petitioned strongly for Georg's release, sending a letter to the Home Secretary Herbert Samuel and visiting the Home Office where he argued personally for Georg's case. Ultimately, Samuel did nothing except refer the case back to the tribunal dealing with internees. In May 1916, with a petition in hand signed by himself and many other well-known writers and artists, John appealed in person to an Advisory Committee in Westminster Hall, but without success (Lilian Sauter to Harrison Morris, May 25, 1916, Princeton University Library). The news about Georg's likely fate, as well as the near-certain fate of Rudolf, made Lilian all the more frail and full of worry. During this period, she sat for a portrait by the artist Leon de Smet who captured her delicate states of body and mind [Figure 21].

Figure 21
Portrait of Lilian Sauter by Leon de Smet, 1916, red and brown crayon with charcoal, 52 x 37 cm. Inscribed in the upper-left corner: "Très respectueusement au cher maître G Sauter, Leon de Smet 6.7.16."
Courtesy of the National Library of Medicine, National Institutes of Health.

Lilian continued to worry even as the police permission she and Rudolf had received, thanks to her brother John, allowed them to travel to Manaton to avoid the anti-German feeling in London where they had been restricted to a five-mile radius of their Holland Park home (Barker 174-175). Anxiety and fear continued to mark their lives through the winter of 1916-17, when, in January, Georg was repatriated to Germany, "able to take nothing with him but his trunk which was robbed on the way & leaving practically all his work locked up in hostile countries" (Lilian Sauter to Harrison Morris, January 21, 1921, Princeton University). Georg and Lilian's love and respect for each other survived "years of mental suffering...of the whole tragedy" of the war, but their marriage did not, since they were unable to reconcile it with Georg's repatriation to Germany (Georg Sauter to Harrison Morris, April 25, 1920, Princeton University Library).

Resilient in the face of the trauma of Georg and Rudolf being interned, as well as her persistent ill-health made worse by her wartime anxiety, Lilian decided to help British women like herself who had married German or Austrian men. She volunteered with the Emergency Committee of the Friends War Victims Relief Committee, visiting German internees in their camps on behalf of their wives and families. She also interviewed families about their circumstances. "In reporting on cases," she reminded herself in her diary, "put: case number, names, and address [on] separate paper for each report" (Cadbury Library, JG(II)/10/6/3).

During the course of her wartime volunteer work, Lilian made the acquaintance of Frieda Ludwig, a musician living in Chiswick who had played piano and sung in concerts held in London's Mary Place (Cadbury Library, JG(II)/10/6/3). In January 1919, the Aliens Advisory Committee of the Home Office named Frieda among "Germans Who May Stay," exempt "from internment or repatriation on the special grounds of long residence in the United Kingdom and well vouched by respectable British subjects" ("Germans Who May Stay"). Lilian was perhaps Frieda's respectable voucher. After the war, the pair became close friends, meeting regularly for social engagements. When Frieda fell gravely ill during the summer of 1924, Lilian composed "Prayer for Frieda":

O God I pray and pray again
Release in this extremity from pain –
Wall round the spirit
    of my friend
With peace, and bring her
    gently to the end.

And after Frieda died the following day, August 14, Lilian addressed her directly:

Frieda
I cannot mourn for you great
hearted Friend -
I can but sing my joy at your
release
that after long drawn months
of pain, the End
Has come, and you our Loved
one are at peace
O Soul of Courage! bearing
endless pain
That to the end the mind
unclouded still
Be prompt to serve, that
none may call in vain
On your great Love and on
your selfless will
O radiant Soul whose Love
made joy, who wrought
With Wisdom to uplift; and
help and free!
Simple of life, noble and broad
in thought
And Loving every beast and
flower and tree
O Frieda, Friend, beloved,
So kind, so true
Live in our hearts that we
may Love Like you.

Later Years

Lilian remained active during her later years despite persistent ill-health, including "a serious operation" in late 1922 which eventually prevented her from travelling overseas (Lilian Sauter to Ethel Fiedler, December 28, 1922, Taylor Institution Library, Oxford University) In addition to composing poetry, she read extensively, wrote letters, gardened, sewed, shopped, made a variety of jams, met friends of tea and dinner, and travelled regionally (Cadbury Library, JG(II)/10/1).

She also sponsored monthly salons as she and Georg had done in their Holland Park home until the war cast its shadow on their lives [Figure 22]. Testifying to her remembrance of those peaceful years, and to her connection to Georg, she kept two different photographs of him in her pocket diary (Cadbury Library, JG(II)/10/1). They still corresponded but never saw each other again. A sullen portrait of Lilian, completed by Rudolf in 1923, belied the many creative, intellectual, political, and social activities she had accomplished by this point in her life [Figure 23].

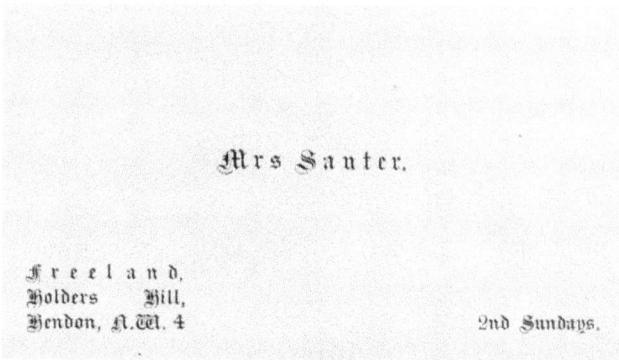

Figure 22
Lilian Sauter's calling card, ca. 1924.
Courtesy of Cadbury Research Library: Special Collections,
University of Birmingham, JG(II)/10/1.

Figure 23
Portrait of Lilian Sauter by Rudolf Sauter, 1923, charcoal on light brown paper,
62.8 x 48.3 cm. Courtesy of Liss Llewellyn Fine Art.

Lilian continued to write in her pocket diaries and read extensively around subjects of religion about which she had contemplated deeply when she was younger (Cadbury Library, JG(II)/10/1). Within the span of two days during August 1924, she completed Rose Macauley's *Told by an Idiot*. By the end of the month, she completed Conrad's first and second novels, *Almayer's Folly* (1895) and *An Outcast of the Islands* (1896), in addition to Elizabeth Robin's *Time is Whispering* (1923) (Cadbury Library, JG(II)/10/1). With the span of two further days, she read Maude Royden's *Prayer as a Force* (1922) and E.M. Forster's *The Longest Journey* (1907). That autumn, perhaps in an effort to revise her earlier thoughts about faith, she read Edward Carpenter's *Pagan and Christian Creeds: The Origin and Meaning* (1920), an attempt to make an objective comparison between the origins and practices of pagan religions and Christianity, and Dennis H. Bradley's *Towards the Stars*, in which the British-born Bradley recounts his experiences with direct voice mediumship he had developed after his experiences with the phenomenon through the American medium George Valiantine (Cadbury Library, JG(II)/10/1).

Shortly before the passing of her friend Frieda, and perhaps with her own mortality in mind, Lilian composed an untitled poem wherein she seemed to embrace anew the creative, independent, intellectual, and loving hallmarks of her life:

I will go up the high green
    down
Removed with the white clouds
    carven crowned
Up to the altars of this Land
under Gods high blue dome
    I'll stand
And sing the Chant of wind
    and sea
And feel the wind blow
    over me
with incense filled and rare
    sweet earth
Wherein the breadth of prayer
    has birth
There I am filled with
    Still Content
Lives in the Souls true
    Element
There I can feel that
    power which gives

Beauty and life to all that
lives
that is in me the power
to Love
To dare, to think, to feel,
to move.

Passing and Burial

On October 27, 1924, nearly two months after her sixtieth birthday,
Lilian died in Freeland. Although she was "ill only one day" before her
passing, she likely fell victim to her longstanding poor health made worse
by the "countless anxieties and sufferings" of the war years combined
with the stress of her marital separation (Gindin, *The English Climate*
161; Georg Sauter to Harrison Morris, December 9, 1919, Princeton
University). All of this, as her sister Mabel later recalled, "had broken
her always frail health, and sapped her powers of resistance. The end
came quickly as the blowing out of a flame." And as Rudolf wrote
to a family friend, "My dear mother passed away quite suddenly and
very peacefully yesterday morning. It was most unexpected although
she had been ill for some time, but her passing was just a quiet as one
could have wished—she slept" (Rudolf H. Sauter to Hermann Georg
Fiedler, October 28, 1924, Taylor Institution Library).[8] Apropos of the
"concrete" life and "eternal verity and death" about which she wrote
in her poem "The Pause," Rudolf produced a memorial card including
this work. He illustrated the card with the same etching of lilies which
had appeared on the first pages of the WWSL leaflet containing her
"Woman's Song of Freedom" and *Through High Windows* (Cadbury
Library, JG(II)/10/3 and 12/2).

Informing its readers about Lilian's passing, the *Evening Standard*
shared that "The world is the poorer by the loss of one very beautiful
character, who had the gift of making life seem a generous thing...
The tiny, fragile figure, always in silver grey, was too frail a
vessel for the great spirit whose unfailing gentleness made her
beloved by all who knew her, or even came within the reach
of her personality...Mrs. Sauter...was author of several slim
volumes of poems of more than ordinary merit. Before the
war, her house in Holland Park-avenue was the rendezvous of
artistic and literary London...
The obituary concluded with a spotlight on her brother John, echoing
the narrative of his famous life which had inhabited the engraved

[8] Rudolf H. Sauter to Hermann Georg Fiedler. 28 October 1924, MS.G/SAUTER
R.1, Taylor Institution Library, Oxford University.

trowel young Lilian used to set the cornerstone of their family home in Coombe Warren fifty-seven years earlier: "Mr. Galsworthy, who was passionately devoted to his sister, is not the only person outside her immediate family who will feel even the autumn sunshine a little sadder to-day, for Lilian Sauter's sake" ("A Beautiful Character"). *The Nottingham Evening Post* did only somewhat better in foregrounding Lilian's own life, experiences, and accomplishments, informing its readers first that she was "the wife of Professor Sauter, the painter… [and] John Galsworthy's sister" and secondly that she was "a poetess of achievement, a frail little woman whose gentle personality was far-reaching in its personal influence" ("Mr. Galsworthy's Loss").

Lilian's family laid her to rest in London's Highgate Cemetery next to her mother and father. On her gravestone, they placed an engraving of the same image of lilies which had appeared on her memorial card, and on the first pages of her "Woman's Highest Plea for Suffrage," published by the Women's Printing Society, and her book *Through High Windows* [Figure 24].

Figure 24
Photograph of the resting place of Lilian Sauter in Highgate Cemetery engraved with the same image of lilies, her namesake flower, which had appeared on her memorial card, and on the first pages of her "Woman's Highest Plea for Suffrage," published by the Women's Printing Society, and her book *Through High Windows*. Photograph courtesy of Mair Salts.

Selected Unpublished Writings (1881-1889)

The Cadbury Research Library, Special Collections, University of Birmingham, holds the largest collection of Lilian's papers as part of its collection of John Galsworthy papers deposited by Rudolf Sauter (Small). Catalogued in this way, Lilian's papers stand within the narrative of her famous brother. On their own and studied in context, they reflect her unique life, personality, and accomplishments. The collection includes the following selected unpublished writings which Lilian either composed directly in, or eventually transcribed to, notebooks dating from the 1880s. Arranged chronologically, these writings are reproduced largely as Lilian composed them. The titles and dates have been edited to achieve consistency in format and, in some instances, clarity in usage of abbreviations and identification of associated locations. Bracketed text indicates Lilian's unclear handwriting and periodic footnotes highlight facts and offer brief background to help readers understand and appreciate the text. In the body of these writings, Lilian's occasional misspellings have been corrected, minor editorial carets taken on board, and formatting regularized to improve the reading experience while still reflecting her intended structure. Nowhere near as polished as her later work, these writings nonetheless help to resurrect Lilian's early voice, creativity, and experiences in and around Coombe, and during her travels to London, Devon, and Brighton. Indeed, they help us to appreciate and understand the creative, curious, independent, and introspective woman and accomplished poet she would come to be, as this introduction has revealed.

Fragment: Begun New Years Eve 1881? in the Blue Room, Coombe Croft[9]

One by one the hours are closing
    Silently the minutes fly.
All things quietly reposing
    Shrouded in the darkness lie
Waiting for the Year to die
Nature throws her snowy covering
    Pure & white on all around
On the air the flakes are hovering
    Silently they kiss the ground
    All is stillness, not a sound!
In my warm house sit I dreaming
    By the endless ruddy glow
Through my brain the thoughts are streaming
    In one swift, continuous flow
    Memories of long ago.
Shadowy phantoms flit before me
    Whispers soft I seem to hear
Loving spirits hover o'er me
    Is it fancy? loved ones dear
    Parted from me long are near!
Happy visions! they have vanished
    Left me sitting here alone
Other thoughts the dreams have banished
    Thoughts of wrong things I have done
    In the year so nearly gone.
Thoughts of resolutions broken
    Actions that have given pain,
Hasty words, & untrue spoken,
    Ne'er to be called back again,
    Thickly throng in Memory's train.

---

[9] The question mark in this title is Lilian's own notation.

Very Early Fragment, about 1883

When the sinking sun, with golden glory
Lightens up the western sky
And the birds their evening hymns are singing
To their Maker up on high
When the distant chimes come floating softly,
Borne upon the evening breeze
And the silver moon is slowly rising
From behind majestic trees.

Written in the garden at Coombe Croft, & never finished

Fragment, begun at a poetry game, one evening at The Leigh[10]

My "question" was, "which talent do you most admire? & my word
forest, I think.

One lovely [? lonely], long September day
O'er woody hills I took my way
And wandered far by bank & brae.

I rambled on as in a dream
Besides a little sparkling stream
Whose ripples caught the sun's last gleam.

Its dancing waters glided by
Reflecting back the golden sky
In every varying brilliancy.

At length a sudden wind it made
And following on through chequered shade
I came upon a sylvan glade.

The forest kings on either side
Majestic reared their heads with pride,
And spread their branches far & wide.

The level sunbeams glinted through
The [beachen?] leaves of amber hue
And on the sward deep shadows drew.

The streamlet now half hid from sight
By fringing fern & lilies white
Went murmuring on with calm delight.

Wooed to repose by all around
Lulled by the brooklet's soothing sound,
I sank upon a grassy mound!

---

[10] Undated but ca. 1881-1883, contemporaneous to her other writings in and
around Coombe Leigh. Lilian noted in her title "M^r [Eleum?], Pritt, & Mr. Nixon
being present I think."

Sweet sleep her spell about me wove,
Yet still I saw the fairy grove
And heard the murmur of the stream
And saw the flickering sunlight gleam
     In my dream.

A gentle breeze swept softly by
Which made the waving branches sigh
The thought it whispered in mine ear,
Look up, a spirit draweth near.

I looked, from out the stream behold
There rose a cloud, & from its fold
Issued the spirit of the air,
A form ethereal, shadowy, fair.

It spoke, & like a distant bell
Soft, but distinct the accents fell
Upon the stillness of the dell,
'Mortal, the choice is thine, choose well.'

My uncarried out idea being to make spirits arise from the stream
& pass before him each representing a talent, from which he was to
choose the loveliest.

Torquay, October 6, 1885 (lines to Mabel)

Lines to Mabel = Forget-me-not,
on her Birthday.

I saw the glorious light of Heaven enfold
A tiny bud, & in its magic hold
The germ of life up sprang, the petals bright
Their arms outspread, received the beauteous light
Within its heart a golden circlet lay
An image of the bright celestial ray,

I watched the tiny floweret as it grew,
Its face upturned reflected Heaven's blue,
A little miror [*sic*] open, true & pure,
An emblem of a faith which shall endure.

Thy Soul O Child 'ere yet thy Father's love
Its wings unfurled, & softly bade it move,
Lay sleeping, like the unopened flower, thou
Canst open all thy heart to love Him now.
Thine eyes uplift to Him, that so His grace
May be reflected too in thy sweet face,
And deep within thy heart's most sacred shrine
Keep bright the image of the Life Divine.
Thy life the outflow of thy love shall be
And thy devotion true to all Eternity.

For thee my heart can wish no happier lot
Than to be ever "GOD's Forget-me-not."

7

Torquay, October 1885, The Passage of the Faithful Soul

Roll, roll, ye Ages, ever backward flee
Towards the abysmal, past Eternity!
Flow back, & in its deep obscurity
O Waves regain your pristine purity!
Sail on, my Bark into Futurity!

Bright veil of morn's sweet prime,
     thou soft'ning dream
Wherein the boundless Heaven & Ocean seem
To blend, & sweet impossibilities
In thousand forms of loveliness arise
To melt & change before mine eager eyes.

I fain would keep thy freshness, but I woo
In vain, thou little film of tender blue!
The faint light quivers into flame, & lo
The wide expanse of Heaven is all aglow,
While pencilled clear, & firm, the outlines
                   flow.

Warm pulses all around me quickening beat!
Thou energising glow of life & heat,
Glory of brightness, flee not yet away,
Nor leave me to the stern-eyed light, & grey,
Of cold Indifference, maturer Day!

Thou current of Opinion, swift & strong
Who barest many an aimless craft along,
I yield not idly to thine influence,
But with the helm of reason & of sense
I stem the tide of thine "Omnipotence"?

Ye in-chains soul-enthralling, break, & fly
Gaunt superstitious, born of mystery,
World fetters, riven by intensest ray
Of thought concentrate, bar no more my way!
Sail on, my Bark, into the freer day.

8

Ye shifting Winds of doubt, without avail
My course ye check, for ye I strike no sail!
Thou Blast of cold unfaith with arrow flight
Of stinging words I bow before thy might,
Awhile, yet rise, & fleeing win the fight.

Fierce rebel waves of passion, rearing high
Your proud white crests against the lowering sky,
In wild defiance of a greater might
Hurled from the treasury of the Infinite,
The Curbing Wind, of high resolve & right.

Be still! the fury of your conflict cease,
O All thou seething waste of waters peace!
Blow steadfast Wind, blow thou & speed my way
False winds, fierce waves, have failed
            and lost their prey
Thee, only thee, my tattered sails obey.

Thou phantom of the watery element,
No cloud on gentle breath from Heaven sent
But vaporous blackness, from the depths untold
Of foulest night uprising, fold on fold,
Thou cruel shroud which dost the light withhold.

Thou utter darkness, palpable & chill
Benumbing e'en the faculty of will,
Thou Child of Hell Despair, I bid thee flee.

I know thee well, yet fear not even thee
Sail on my Bark into the open sea!!

Ye rocks, far-looming on the awful main,
Or sunk in treacherous Shadow, wait in vain,
In vain with peaked head ye cleave the skys
In vain your deep deceptive shadows lie,
Sail on my Bark, & glide securely by.

Stern heights of Sorrow, though I thread your gloom
Flung, where around me, lurketh many a tomb,
What tho' ye lead me to the Vast Unknown,
Thro' gates which clang the echoes "pass, alone",
Without a fear I sail serenely on.

9

One silver thread across the trackless deep
Hath served my Bark upon her course to keep,
A single narrow track of mystic light,
Which shineth clearest in the depth of night,
Unfathomable, pure, & wondrous bright.

Unwavering still, tho' many years have flown,
Since o'er the waters sped one Bark, alone,
Cleaving the terrors of a path untried,
Scanning its trail, a never failing guide,
Wherein who sail, may ever safely ride.

I follow still thro' portals decked with woe,
I feel a thrill, I see that bright stream glow,
And widen, till a darkly rolling flood,
Of awful depth,—[measures] a sea of blood—
It bears me onward into bliss untold,
Its dark waves merging in a sea of gold.

O greatly longed for Heaven of calm rest,
Take me awhile to thine unruffled breast,
That freed from all the carking ills of care
My shattered Bark may find her full repair
Till to perfection so her form be wrought,
That she express once more her Maker's
                              thought,
And in His Presence rest, for evermore,
The image of that Bark that went
                              before.

Teignmouth, October 1885 (for Châtelaine)

Dreams.
Oh who can fully fathom & explain
        The wonderous action of the sleeping brain?
The strange, fantastic flitting, of the mind
        That leaves all sense of time & place behind
And wanders aimless through a sunny maze
        Of far off scenes, & dim remembered days.
Mingling sweet memories; And who would dare
        To curl that Pegasus, or cleans the air
Where midst the cloud-like realms of phantasy
        Sports wild Imagination trammel-free.

Whence come the forms we never yet have seen!
        The combinations that have never been?
Who weaves the chain of thought so close & bright
        So airy that it crumbles with the light
Are they creations of the unfettered soul?
        Or of the body freed from its control?
Or are they outward visions of the night
        Spirits, made visible to mortal sight?
Unknown their source, but more sumptuous [?] still
        The mission they are destined to fulfil.

The sudden motion of a quick descent
        The tangled meshes of bewilderment,
Through which the fancy feebly tries to thread,
        The chilling horror of a nameless dread,
For these no higher cause has man assigned
        Than action of the body on the mind.

But scenes there are, which to the mental eye
        Stand out defined with clear intensity,
Deeds wrought in secret, by the unknown dead,
        Are reenacted, filling us with dread.
Or yet again, a radiant form we see,
        Luring to, warning us from, Destiny.

11

Or, in a moment of untold despair,
　　　When grief is too intense for soul to bear,
The cloud which veils the future from its sight
　　　Rolls back, revealing, thro' the depths of night
Vistas of joy, immeasurably bright.

Such dreams, however they come, are surely sent,
　　　Straight from the Mind of GOD, The Armament
Of Heaven with weapons such as these is strong
　　　To battle for the right, to quell the wrong.
And 'tis a thought of reassurance sweet,
　　　A thought our minds in childhood leapt to meet
That loving spirits round our footsteps wait
　　　To carry all our needs to Heaven's Gate.

Torquay, October, 1885 (for Châtelaine)

Autumn
Autumn leaves, crisp & dead
Swiftly fall,
O'er the earth lightly spread
Summer's pall
Sunlight weaves golden thread
Overall.

Gleams of fleet, quivering light
Glint & stray,
Deck with gems, in their flight,
Every spray.
Trails of gold, burnished bright,
Gently sway.
Many a dark, shadow wreath
Frets the ground
Keen & fresh, Heaven's breath
Stirs around
Full of events born of Death
Full of sound.

Streams of joy on th'intent
Ear outflow,
Welling forth sweet content,
All aglow
With what love Heavenward sent
None can know.

Summer's touch, softer grown
Lingers, where
'Gainst the dark pine here thrown
Emerald fair,
Tender leaves, yet unflown
Wave in air.
Amber soft, flings her veil,
Fluttering bright
Russets dark melt in pale

Auburn light
Fiery burns many a trail
On the sight.

Berries bright, overhead
Hanging high,
Bramble leaves, blushing red
Claim the eye,
Rubies Shine 'neath the tread
Modestly.

Every sweet growing thing
Every hue
All the clear notes that ring,
Glad & true
Tell of Him whence they spring
And the Soul worshipping
Breathes anew:

O Thou, from Whose deep Heart
All beauty springs,
Thou, Beauty's self Who art,
Past all imaginings;
Essence Divine;
Flow through this life of mine,
That it may be with Thine
In harmony
That so each beauty here
May but the shade appear
My GOD, of Thee!

Birthday Lines to Father, November 23, 1885

The Leigh, Coombe

Father! I love to think the name,
And in my secret heart enthrone
    The form it brings.
Father! I love the word to frame
It strikes a chord of sweetest love
    On Memory's strings.

A Chord whose every note hath thrilled
With love full many a time my soul
    And wakened there
An echo; you whose sound hath stilled
The distant unmelodious roll
    Of dull despair.

Soft notes faint quivering through the past
In full crescendo swelling clear
    And clearer yet.
Undying notes whose sound shall last
To sweeten memory year by year
    And soothe regret;

Of Self-less deeds, in patience wrought,
Which half the loving care reveal
    And veil the woe
Which brought them forth; of anxious thought
Which compasseth another's weal
    With many a throe;

Of sudden sympathy which flings
A silent greeting from the heart,
    A subtle spell,
O bright with kindling word up springs
To meet the trembling step of Art
    And guide it well;

Of brave forbearance, tender-strong
With pettyness of feebler minds;
  Of honour clear,
Of moral strength to own a wrong,
Scattering opinion to the Winds
  Devoid of fear;

Ye from a Father's life outflow
In harmony of love, divine
  —The sweetest music heart can know
Mingle, & enter into mine.

Sweet Melody, thy source how dear
Long mayst Thou gladden with thy strain
The wearied heart, the wistful ear,
And quietly soothe the cry of pain.

And may the echoes waked by thee
In our young souls with gathering might
In flood of fuller harmony
Around our Father's life unite.

Birthday Lines to Mother, December 6, 1885

The Leigh, Coombe

Mother, words are cold & breath is fleeting
That would fain my burning thought convey
Only words of old familiar greeting
Through my lips in wishful accents stray
"Many happy comings of today."

Mother, words are few & thoughts are thronging
Deep & tender, full of love & woe,
Full of deep unutterable longing
All the sympathy of love to know.

Mother, times there are of silent weeping,
When from years afar, on Memory's wing
Thoughts of mingled joy & sorrow, sweeping
O'er the soul, its every fibre wring.

When the waves of vain regret are flowing
O'er the crumbled shrine of days gone by
And the debt of love, for ever owing.

Then, messieurs, my love was love more real
When in child life round thy form entwined
It adored in thee, a bright ideal,
And, a perfect living, thee enshrined.

Seems it that as faded out the splendour
Of the softning unreality
Faded something too of love, the tender
Light died out in dull formality.

Seems it only, in a moments blindness
Fraught with pain, on evil whispers borne,
Then I turn me to thy loving kindness
Mother darling, all my hardness gone.

Mother, see, my love for thee is weavéd
With my very life, & cannot die,
Though awhile of childhoods faith bereavéd
Knitted close, with immortality.

It is there, tho' other threads are flying,
Though unwoven, other colours twine,
Ever strongest, brightest, underlying
Every other love, that love of thine.

Though to rue in clearer light revealéd
Shines thy womanhood, in frailty 'rayed
Thou art dearer, for the dim concealéd
Depths of love & sweetness in its shade.

And the very weakness, closely binding
Soul to soul, in sympathy is sweet,
Each in others some refreshment finding,
When in free conceding love they meet.

Oft beneath the veil of cheerful seeming
Shrinking sorrow lurketh all unseen,
And we wound it sorely, little dreaming,
In our blindness, how our words are keen.

Need of love is sore at times & growing
All unheeded, and the hearts great deep,
Scarce were filled tho' love were always
                       flowing
Tho' the fount of love could never sleep.

Then in strong forbearance Gentle Mother
Keeping sympathy for ever bright
Let us all unwearied help each other
Till our love be perfected in Light.

A Christmas Wish to Mother, 1885

The Leigh, Coombe (Châtelaine)

Love in every Christmas token
      Glisten forth to meet thine eye
Smile in every face unspoken,
      In each word of greeting lie.

Fill thy home with Christmas gladness
      Fill thy heart with holy peace,
Banish every trace of sadness
      Bid all sound of sorrow cease
Love, the theme of Angel Story
      Love, the link twixt life & death,
Love which left a Heaven of glory
      To make sweeter sorrow's breath.

Love, the Gift of GOD in Christmas tide
      Shed Its living Presence far & wide
Blessing all thy life, with Angel wing
      All thy future way o'ershadowing.

To Father with Gift of New Bradshaw[11]

Christmas 1885, The Leigh

May trains no more perplex thee
And Figures no more vex thee,
Bradshaw, "old & tried"
Still be he thy guide!
That worthy friend
His ways shall mend
At least his <u>shabby</u> ways have end.
'Neath cover new
Well hid from view
His foibles hide,
In decent pride
Don't look inside
Until you must
But blindly trust
And kindly say, without delay
Like Roberts at the Mascotte play
"O Bradshaw, I annex thee."

---

[11] "Bradshaw" refers to Bradshaw's series of railway timetables and travel guidebooks.

The Leigh, December 1885 (for Châtelaine)

A Christmas Lyric.
Angel Feathers, soft, descending
        Flakes of pure, unsullied snow
Weave your veil, in mystery blinding
        All above with all below.

Robe the earth in virgin whiteness
        All unloveliness conceal
And arrayed in glistering brightness
        Every graceful form reveal.

Deep in death-less silence folding
        All the World, in chill suspense,
Nature breathless stilly holding
        As with waitful thought intense.

Faint upon the silence stealing
Let the joy-bell sweetly ring,
Clearer, louder ever, pealing
        Forth the advent of our King.

For in mystic, joyous meeting
        Mercy upon Truth hath smiled
While with Peace in holy greeting
        Righteousness is reconciled.

All th'ineffable effulgence
        Of an awful Purity
All too pure to shed indulgence
        On a stained humanity.

And the yearning, wondrous tender
        Of a love of depth undreamed
In divinest self-surrender
        On a world of sin that gleamed,

Mingled in one pure life filling
  With a glory all the earth
Hearts with loving rapture thrilling
  At the sinless Saviour's birth.

Here let all the earth adoring
  Welcome, and with sweet accord,

Many voiced or still outpouring
  Praises, worship Him as Lord.

Let our hearts be pure before Him
  On this holy Christmas Morn
To receive Him & adore Him
  Who for us in love was born.

Kensington Palace Mansions

June 1886

To Helene
There is no thought of love, no still delight
Which wakes my heart to secret extasy
No vision that enchains the inward sight
But therewith mingles some sweet
thought of thee.
No wish for present life my heart can frame,
No yearning for the higher life Divine,
No wonder at the life that none can name,
The after Death, but has a link
with thine.

Kensington Palace Mansions,
Thoughts of a Cartesian Sceptic[12]

When I have dared to question 'are things so?'
To look a dogma in the face & say
'Art thou, whom all men deem the truth, a lie?'
Then have I struck the first defiant blow
For mental freedom, & a little way
Around me [cleared]. But by that blow am I
Dissevered from this faith I held so dear,
Dissevered, mind & mind from friend & kin
Free, but in awful solitude of doubt
To wrestle with my dim discernéd fear,
To still the warring elements within
To heal the broken harmonies without.

Sealed by that blow are all my future years
To patient toil & unremitting strife
To rescue truth from error? Be it so,
Were every sympathy dissolved in tears
And peace for ever fled, & all my life
A struggle, I would bless that sacred blow.

For not the thought of joy untouched by pain,
Unventured safety, nor the even flow
In thoughts untroubled days twist mind & [mind]
Can dim the bright assurance that I gain
Of deeper joys beyond me, & below
A firmer ground of safety, & to find

That Truth, for which I seek, is not afar.
But all around, within me growing clearer,
A unifying Principle, divine
Uniting things that were, with things that are;
It is to find a sympathy far dearer
Than any sympathy that erst was mine.

---

[12] Undated but ca. 1887, contemporaneous to her other poems composed in and around Kensington Palace Mansions.

Kensington Palace Mansions, June 7, 1886

2/6 worth of noise & trouble.
Our 1ˢᵗ & last experience of the upper gallery at a Richter Concert,
Wagner Night.

We started on that fateful day
While yet the world in sunshine lay,
And having dined on fish & tea
A quite delightful treat to me,
We felt distinctly 'fit' & said
We'd have a hansom cab instead
Of stifling in a growler, so
We hail a hansom, & we go.
The London Streets were all aflow
With people hurrying to & fro,
A vast, & ceaseless surging sea
Of many wheeled humanity.
Our little horse, not over fleet
Threaded with care the busy street,
We passed the Park, where wealth & rank
Were whisking in & out then sank
Our hearts, for lo the crowd was great!
And there we had to stand & wait,
Up Piccadilly then to crawl
With prospect of no seat at all
In over filled Sᵗ. Jameses Hall,
We reached at last our destination
And in the passage took our station
A crowd already was assembled
The which I looked upon & trembled
We had not stood a moment there
Before we felt the need of air,
For close behind us thick & fast
The people crowded till at last
It really was so warm, I felt,
Another moment, I should melt!
But after 15 minutes frying
When I was just resigned to dying

25

The crowd in front began to move,
The folk behind to pike & shove,
They trod upon my heels, alack,
They made a hole in Mother's back.
A false alarm!, no door unclosed
As we in melting hope supposed ----
The conversation flowed around,
It had a rather cockney sound,
It savoured of the vulgar mind,
Of bread & cheese, scarce left behind!
At last! the sounds of opening greet
Our ears, & spur our nimble feet,
We struggle up the stony flights
That lead to unexplored heights
We do our best to lose our way
And only chafe at each delay.
We tread with care another's toes,
To take advantage of his woes,
And gain a step, at least <u>some</u> do,
I hear one boasting of it too.
We reach the final stage at last,
But yet the crisis is not past,
Upon a seat we promptly sit,
Wherein but one can rightly fit,
Rising with haste, we seek in fear,
Two other places, find them near,
And sink exhausted on a seat
Conscious of nothing but the heat.
While rises all around the din
Of flocks of people, settling in,
And shouts of "programme, one a shilling"
And greetings many, far from chilling
I hear my left hand neighbour's puns!
My right-hand neighbours catch buns
I wither with innate disdain,
I never shall touch buns again!
The seats are small, the backs are straight
<u>My</u> back is formed to undulate
Nor will it easily compose
Itself to stiffness in repose
For full an hour we have to sit!
My Mother wishes she could knit,
While I resort to writing this,

To mitigate my perfect bliss!
My Father now appears behind,
A single seat he cannot find.
His face, if I can read it right
Expresses far from pure delight
In this refreshing atmosphere
The reason I perceive, t'is clear
The grapes are sour, I tell him so,
He takes a plunge for seats below,
The time is up, Herr Haus is late,
They really should begin at 8.
Meanwhile a most unholy sound,
A kind of "having razors ground"
Ascends, & fills me with a groan,
Oh where alas! is Mendelssohn?
Who ne'er allowed his men the check
Of making one untuneful squeak.
They come, they come, the [donnas?] 2
The one in pink, the other blue,
The tenor, bass, & baritone
Are in their place, but 10 to 1
I haven't any ear left, Oh!
The clapping doth offend it so!
Alas, mine ear, what din arises,
What new & horrible surprises!
What clash of [shimmered?] pots & pans,
What creaking of o'erladen vans,
With jingling bells, & clarions shrill,
And thunder from 'Olympian Hill',
And, above all melodious, yell,
Which nought can stifle, nought can quell!
The intentions of this sound are good!!
It would inform us if it could
The way to love with all our might,
Without a thought of faith, & right!
The way to meet in secret bowers,
And joy in such unholy hours!
It does its best of love to tell:
The voices lower their dreadful yell,
The trumpets cease, the creaks & groans
Sigh in unheard of, broken, tones.
A wind gets up, & shakes the sky,
And waves the branches noisily!

And makes you feel inclined to cry,
Nay, brings the hopes of melody;
(Not to the point, all this, but nice)
When, full of terrors, in a trice
It rises to a shreak again,
And Peace, has tried it on in vain!

This is the fashion of the day!
    This is a music past compare,
For this will mortals fight their way,
    And spend an hour upon the stair!
To this will they expose their ear,
    For this in suffering patience wait.
Breathing a loathesome atmosphere
From 7 of the clock till 8.

    Mem:
Selection: Act 2 Tristan & Isolde, & meeting
of Siegfried & Brunhilde
Vocalists : Fraŭlein [Maltese?] &
& Jorren Henschel & Gudehus.

These lines are not intended as the expression of my opinion of Wagner's music in general, but of this particular selection, nor to cast any slur on the orchestration which was exquisite throughout, but merely to give a faint idea of its effect, under such trying circumstances.

Thought, "in the dawning of a bright Spring day" at the Leigh, Coombe

written [at] Kensington Palace Mansions, June 1886

To Helene.
Earth wakes from death
    Soft murmureth
    Her virgin breath
With sweetest odours rife
    While far & near
    Bright things appear
    And softly clear
[Outswell] the notes of life.

A holy light
    Which crowns the flight
    Of (hideous) Night   (or sable)
In haste investeth all
    With tenderest hue
    Of quivering blue
    And all things new
Beneath her magic fall.

    One star benign
    From crystal shrine
    With kiss divine
Doth greet the smiling day
    While glistereth yet
    The dew [gem] set
    In violet
Or budding hawthorn spray.

Love wakes without, in Beauty's dawn on earth
With silent shout, she hails the springs new birth
Love wakes within, Love shakes her pinions free
Love wakes! and in her freshness
                    soars to thee.

September 1886, Ashburton

After a drive with Father & Mother over the Moor, in all its sunlit glory of purple & gold; & a birthday picnic on [Honister] Tor with the Buckleys in a mist![13]

Dartmoor:
Oh how I love thy hills of rippled gold,
And purple-shadow, soft'ning fold & fold!
Thy blinding hues of bracken, gorse & ling,
Thy wild, wild, birds forever on the wing.
I love, nay I could kiss the heather sweet,
That springs, scarce bent beneath my wing'ed feet,
& blesses all thy life-inspiring breath
With fragrance, aye I love the bonny heath
Freely I revel in thy freshness keen,
Thy unbreathed sweetness; what repose to lean
Upon thy bare & craggéd strength, mine eye
Banging thy space, To me tis bliss to lie
& watch the soft, free clouds o'er Heaven sweeping,
Here sunlit smiling, yonder gently weeping,
Clotting with transient richness, depth & light
Thy never changing hills. How warm & bright
They lie, those golden billows! Stay, behold
How soft & blue! Anon how darkly cold
and lowering! Touched as with a magic wand
By the cloud-pencils of a Master-Hand!
What is there in the World so fraught with joy,
So absolutely free from all alloy
So bright, so tireless in variety
As every sparkling rill that wells from thee,
& o'er the heather winds its limpid way
To break o'er rocky beds in rainbow spray
Endowing myriad life with rich delight
& filling Earth with music exquisite.
Where is the pomp & splendour I can name
With all thy glory, when the Western Flame
[Flashes] thy purple domes with ruddy glow,

[13] The Buckleys refers to the family of Blanche Buckley. See note the poem "To Blanche Buckley," below.

Flooding with liquid are the lands below.
Wan as the primrose fading in the sky
Behind the rugged gloom & majesty
Of thy grand Tors, the kingly Sentinels
Of that far golden land where daylight dwells,
Where can the sense of terror so overwhelm
As in the bleakness of thy untrod realm
When sweeps the breath of Winter, keen & rude
Across thy snowy breast; & solitude
And Silence, deathlike, o'er the darkness brood
Thus awe-inspiring know I not thy land
Yet what, on Earth unutterably grand
As thou, when from thy farthest verge arise
All blue-of-[Ind ?] the mantles of the skies,
& silver phantom-clouds like spirits glance

Against their sombre pile, in sprightly dance
While all the canopy of Heaven is bright
With weird, mysterious, glow of saffron light!
Then wakes the voice of Heaven, muttering deep
& low, in thy far hills, where thunders sleep,
& rolls from tor to tor, from Coombe to Coombe
Like thousand voices swelling from the tombe,
& breaks, in triumph pealing to the sky
In one grand chord, exultant 'ere it die.
I love, thy storm wrought moods, & silent bow
Before the grandeur of thy folded brow.
Before the Presence thron'ed on thy hills
With awe & love my inmost being thrills.
Land of the Dart, my soul is knit to thee
By memories of shadowless delight,
By glimpses of a life as pure & free
As thy free Winds in their unfettered flight.
By those deep longings thou hast ever stirred
For something higher, nobler more akin
To thine own infinite beauty, in a word
For Deity! & by that sense within
The hearts deep solitude, of peace divine,
And rest, which flows from contemplating thee
And all the strength & beauty w[hic]^h are thine,
By these my heart is bound eternally,
For these I thank thee lovely land & dwell
In thought with thee when far away,
                                    Fare well!

31

October 1, 1886, Ashburton

The "Vale of Tears."

A chamber wrapped in gloom of still despair
A girlish form, beside a pallet kneeling,
Praying with heart & soul, a voiceless prayer,
Bowed with a sorrow none but she is feeling,
"None in the World" she thinks, but she "can know
Such anguish, not another loves him so."

His soul is straining at the tender strings
That fetter it to life, it w[oul]ᵈ be free,
It longs to soar beyond imaginings,
It longs to grasp the hand of Certainty.
"Great GOD,"—she prays "hold yet Thy hand for see
He has no wings to bear his soul to Thee."

O bitterness of parting!, depth of woe!
The sting has pierced, she grasped it all in vain,
The sting of parting, is it not to know
That soul & soul can never meet again!
That one whom we would forfeit all to save
Must flutter faithless down, beyond the grave.

"Is there no thought, no sympathy divine
With this my sorrow, is there none to hear?
O Saviour, answer, tell me he is Thine!
My soul is wrestling with a deadly fear,
Could I but feel him happy, could I know
That He had found Thee, I could let him go."

Wan as the Vestal of a storm-clad sky,
& all as pure & full of tender grace
With clouds of grief o'ercast, appealingly
Upturned to Heaven is that angel face
Her eyes are gleaming, thro' a mist of tears
Into the dim expanse of by-gone years.

And in that far recess she seems to be
Again with him she loves, in union blest,
By some inexplicable sympathy
A moment as in mutual wonderment
They gaze upon the work of one who wrought
To shape with painter's skill a poet's thought.

It stretches now, before her tranc'ed eyes,
Ah now she seems to tread its sacred gloom,
On either hand the barren heights arise
Casting around the twilight of the tomb;
She trembles in her loneliness & fears
The desolation of the "Vale of Tears."

A Vale of tears in very truth, for see,
At every turn a group of human woe,
The very air is thick with misery;
With every proud distinction trampled low,
The crown'ed grief, the raimentless [?] despair,
The sick the lone, the sin-struck, meet her there.

x Dorés "Vale of Tears."
A rainbow glory breaks athwart the haze,
A gentle Presence steals upon the sight,
A hand is stretched the drooping form to raise,
A countenance with kindred feeling, bright,
A hope on every aching brow distils
And with a Christlike peace, the spirit fills.

On that calm, seraph-wing'ed glance is borne
Love inexpressible & infinite
Within her spirit, sorrow-crushed & worn,
In commune deep, it, thus, dispells her night;
"O Child of little faith, & views confined,
Love with a love which filleth all thy Mind.

Casting out fear, nor dream that he who clings
With love sincere, tho' blind, who strives to see,
The hand he clings to, who has lost the wings
Of faith, & can but stagger after me,
Is to my heart less infinitely dear,
Than her who swiftly treads a path more clear."

November 1, 1886, Kensington Palace Mansions

Thine eyes are weary for the glow
Of Autumn on the waving land,
My feet, impatient long to spring
On Devon's smooth elastic strand.
Thine ear <u>will</u> strain to catch the flow
Of silver notes on either hand
In vain,—The blue sea murmuring
Sweet music to the snowy sand
Beneath the soft red cliffs can send me not
Its "hush" & "flow" to this unrestful spot.

A tarnished thread of Autumn's gold
Falls, as her mantle rustles by,
She stays, to wreathe it 'mong the trees,
To smile a smile, & breathe a sigh
& leaves thy gaunt elms bare & cold,
["Chemsiton" ?], while drearfully
Her sign moans like the wintry breeze
Her smile shines, faintly, tearfully;
In pity for the weary London eyes,
That may not see her riches treasuries.

The ceaseless ebb & flow of life
Fills with a muffled din the air,
With here a quavring coster-cry;
An organ note discordant there,
My heart with restless feelings rife,
Looks out on hurry, grief, & care
And longs for peace, & wearily
I thread the crowded thorougfare.
<u>Such</u> is the City's shore, the London "Strand",
Where waves of pain & joy meet hand to hand
Or look I forth at early day
Into the "Gardens", grim forlorn
Thick, yellow night is falling quickly,
A yellow night at early morn!!
The giant leafless elms loom grey,
Against a pallid yellow sky,

As tho' a sun were setting sickly
Into a southern grave. Thine eye
Beholds an elfin forest, weird & strange,
A phantom world where restless spirits

        range,

Stay! there is beauty in this night!
A strange, weird stilness, as of death,
A momentary, welcome hush;
Aye, there is vigour in the breath
Of Autumn, & her tears are bright,
Even as on London brows they fall
There is a music in the rush
Of many feet, aye, after all
A solemn, stirring, soul enthralling strain
Throbs from the heart of grief & care & pain.
The notes from out some heart made free
That swell, the glance of brightened eye,
Are worth the seas soft murmuring!
Its sparkle neath the sunny skies!
For who can hear, & do, & see,
Are op'ed the secret treasuries
Of beauty never dim; the spring
Of love & joy that never dies.
So ["Deven"?], even would I rather be
With sobre, weary London, than with thee

        (Châtelaine)

November 23, 1886, Father's Birthday

To Father,
As, like An Autumn Violet, the Year
    O Silver-Crowned behind [thee] dies,
Like odours sweet, may memories
    Enfold thee in a balmy atmosphere.

As in this light of Autumn's mellow rays
    A [gem] bedews its petal sere,
So glistening on the fading Year
    May be the tears of thankfulness & praise.

As fades the violet, again to spring
    In other forms of beauty, so
May the dead year regretless go,
But to return with richer blossoming
    or thus:
As in the waning year the violet dies
Giving out life, with sweet perfumèd sight
Begemmed with dews that starlike shimmer
Beneath the faint sun's fitful glimmer,
As, into earth it sinks, again to rise
With fuller odours, fresher colouries.

So may the dying year exhale for thee,
O Silver Crowned, the balm of memory,
With thankful tears bedewed & gleaming
In rays from Heaven's glory streaming.
So, in oblivion may it sink, to be,
With fuller, richer joys returned to thee.

December 1, 1886, lines on text,
"And makes Thy chosen People Joyful"

O GOD we life our hearts to Thee!
Of every time, in ever land
A chosen but a secret band
     To Thee
In lonely prayer we bend the knee.

Thou knowest whose are Thine alone,
     O Thou to Whose attentive ear
     The Sinners cry is music, hear
     And own
The prayer ascending to Thy throne.

O Mercy! of unsung renown.
     To whom the tear of Penitence
     Outshines the diamonds radiance
     Stoop down
And gather tear gems for Thy crown.

O Purity! & Truth! divine
     The deadly struggle with our sin
     The strife for purity within
     Are Thine!
O on our feeble efforts shine.

Omniscience Who alone canst see
     The pain of heart & secret woe
     Which we to mortal may not show
     To Thee
In all our trouble may we flee.

O Lord the source of joy, the spring
     Of deathless gladness, let it flow
     That we, thy chosen here below
     May sing
Thy Matchless praise, Almighty King.
                      (Châtelaine.)

My First Sonnet

Kensington Palace Mansions, December 31, 1886

To Helene
The moments lengthen into hours, & days.
That Part us hand from hand & eye from eye,
And distance baffles e'en the mental gaze
And stills my word of greeting to a sigh
Ere it can wing its eager flight to thee
O for the freedom of the wild sweet "West"
To seep in music over land & sea,
And whisper soft my greeting "[in German, illegible]," or in silence
   now,
To weave a wreath of cloud above thy way,
And drop a gentle kiss upon thy brow,
Then, let the sunbeams through my cloud wreath play
Till every drop dissolve & Heaven's beam
Emblem of Heaven's Love, upon thee gleam.

New Year's Eve 1886-1887

Holy & bright,
Star-lit, & still, is the beautiful Night!
Down thro' the deepening, fathomless blue,
Swiftly & true
Shimmer the rays from her crescent-light.

Diamond Sheen
Lightly encrusteth her Vesture green.
Dark is the shadow, purple & brown
Sable-lined gown
Folding her close from a breath too keen.

Breathless & white
Shiv'ring & cold is the beautiful Night
Bidding the year that she knows, fare well!
(Hark 'twas a knell!)
Watching to speed him his last, sad flight.

Hark! from afar!
Ringing of love to the morning-star
Ringing out pain, as their music swells
Hark to the bells!
Ringing in hope that shall live for aye,
Welcoming sweetly the fair new day.
                    (Châtelaine.)

8 Cambridge Gate, January 29, 1888

Dedicated to "The Preacher"

In grateful mem[ory of] Sundays, Jan 8-15, 1888
the following parody—

After Dr. Watts' ''Tis the voice of the [Sluggard]'
By a 'Mr. Orthodox'

T'was the voice of the Preacher, I heard him explain
'You have broken the Sabbath again & again,'
'You obey a command to keep <u>one</u> day for <u>rest</u>
'By keeping <u>another</u> as you may think best!'

2.
'The Sabbath Commandment was given to the <u>Jews</u>,
'And had <u>nothing to do</u> with a pulpit, & pews.
'It was never enforced by a Christian decree,
'And as to its import, few sects can agree!'

3.
'<u>Let</u> <u>us</u> <u>know</u>' said the Preacher, 'at least what we <u>mean</u>
'When our Sunday array of best bonnets is seen?
'Away with a vain, superstitious <u>pretence</u>!
'For which you have never a shade of defence!'

At this point I felt it incumbent upon me
as a good Churchman, to walk out.

4.
I passed by his pulpit, & marked with some care
That no Sunday observance had silvered his hair,
The <u>gown</u> that hung on him, it grieves me to say
Showed no signs of being worn more than once in the day.

40

5.

I wrote him a letter, neat, polished & terse,
Said 'I hoped I might never hear anything worse,
of that had I expected heretical jeers
I'd have brought cotton wool & have stuffed up my ears!'

6.

I challenged an answer, but Heaven knows why,
My anonymous letter obtained no reply –
I penned him another, he still was unshaken
By all my endeavours to prove him mistaken!

7.

I paid him a visit, still hoping to find
That my words had induced him to alter his mind,
But he asked me, a Churchman, (imagine my shrinking!)
'Had I studied my Bible, or ever tried thinking?'

8.

Controlling my feelings, I asked 'did he find
The observance of Sunday was bad for mankind
He replied, 'not at all, it is good on the whole
'To combine the refreshment of body & soul'

9.

I remarked, 'the observance you did not defend
In your sermon!' Said he, 'did you wait for the end?'
'The value of worship I've never denied,
'Nor that worship, & rest, may be placed side by side.

10.

'But to base the connection, I think you have heard
'On the Sabbath Com[andment] is wholly absurd'!!-
I took up my hat, for remonstrance was vain,
And mentally vowed not to call [thus/there] again

11

Said I then to my friends, 'It's appalling to see
Such heretical fools at the top of the tree.
I shall write to the [pagans/papers?] declaring my views
And I heartily hope they may empty his pews.

12

But one, with a feeling of secret delight

41

Who had watched from a corner the disputants' flight
Spoke then to the Preacher = "I think I may say
That the narrow-church party'd the Worst of the fray."

13
But O logical friend! can you truly deny
That on ground very broad, a connection does lie
Betwixt the enforcement of rest on mankind
& the Worship therewith for long ages combined?

14
For, to question the aim of repose, as we can,
Is it not the Refreshment, the quickening of man?
& what, then, is man? Spirit, Intellect, Will,
To refresh but the body is not to fulfil

15
In all its intention far-reaching & grand,
Nay, scarce to the letter, the Sabbath Command.
Recreation of soul is to exercise due,
While that of the body to rest, it is true.

16
"But we also admit, 'tis the nature of things,
"That refreshment from Change of activity springs
Not only from rest, to the over wrought flame,
Nay, it may be that rests but a word for the same

17
I cannot help thinking, it may be I'm wrong,
That God meant "Refreshment" by "Rest" all along,
That we cannot read into forms He has given,
A meaning more broad than was thought of in Heaven

18
If even in Moses His Mouthpiece of old
No view of their unity yet could unfold—
If still to the multitude "worship" & "rest"
On the 1st & the 4th, two Commandments at best,

19.
To you & to me, they are merged in one Will:
"Get thee Ready for work, gather life to thy fill

"Arise, in thy manhood, <u>Mind</u>, <u>body</u>, & <u>soul</u>
"And worship thy maker, who maketh thee whole.

20.

"My friend is this so? Are we tired, are we vexed
And has "worship" <u>then</u> <u>Nothing</u> to do with your text?"
The Preacher looked up with a gleam of surprise
And a very broad twinkle appeared in his eye

21.

"Neatly put; with your view I entirely agree,
"But with half your acuteness t'were easy to see
"That in every Command the whole Decalogue lies
"Yet to Preach <u>one</u> Command <u>at a time</u> – <u>may</u> be <u>wise</u>."

22.

The way of the Preacher O Who would desire!
It leads from the frying pan into the fire!
And I am not a man who would butter the pan,
Or relinquish my aim at the breath of the flame!

November 18, 1888, Belvedere Mansion, Brighton

Clear the wide sky
  Blue the bright sea
Heaven draweth nigh
  O my love, with thee.
Light the clouds fly,
  Blow the winds free,
Left the long depth
  Of the freshening sea.

Swift the clouds merge
  Moan the winds low
Wild the waves surge
  On the rocks below.

Rage of fierce sound
  Blackness above
Death is around
  Thee my love, my love.

Dawns the grey light
  Swell the calm sea;
Ah! for the sight
  That were Heaven to me!

Keep him, Oh keep—
  Thou who didst take
Let him not [weep]
  For his bride's sweet sake.

Yet in Thy sight
  Keep him for me,
Lead me aright
  Who for tears scarce see.

Help me to do
  Help me to love
Let me be true
  Till we meet above!

Slow the days gather,
    Death cometh late.
Help me O Father
    Help me to wait!

For My Father, November 23, His Birthday, 1888

God give thee joy,
and fill thy year with blessing.
Beyond my deepest wish thy days with gladness fill
Far from [annoy],
From pain or fear oppressing
Keep He thy Cherished life with His almighty Will.

We can not know,—
So feeble our divining,—
The future store He gathers there of good or ill –
This yet we trow,
That be it veiled or shining
The love that grows not dim in Heaven is o'er thee still.

E'en if His love,
Which willeth thy redeeming
From breach of love which bind thy narrow self to [Him?]
'Till grief should move
To every outward seeming—
And care should overwhelm & outward pleasures flee.

God give them peace
And heart-secure Relying,
On Him who knoweth all, who doeth all things well.
Care then shall cease,
Desire & sorrow dying
For where He giveth peace Can never trouble dwell.

"When He giveth quietness Who then can make trouble"
Job, 35.29—

8 Cambridge Gate, December 11, 1888

1.

What shall I say that is new when all things are told?
[Lives?] there a thought so true as ne'er to be old?
Breathes there a sound so sweet we would hear it again
Heard tho' it be in a moment of languor & pain?

2.

Aye there is one sweet thought that for ever is young,
One little sound that is soft on the harshest tongue.
Down in the grief dried heat it falls like dew,
Feeding the springs of life that they flow anew—

3.

<u>Love</u>, is a young, young thought, with a name as old—
Old, as the fields that lie in a sheet of gold—
Even in spring the same, yet ever new
Such is your love for me, & mine for you.

To Blanche Buckley, On Her Leaving Kingillie,
August 12, 1889[14]

As the wide moor without the heather
Chill, colourless & bare,
As the blank day in Highland weather
When mist drops felt the air
As the wild sky when clouds are flying
Out to a sunless West
As the dull hearth where embers dying
A vanished warmth attest—

E'en so a house where though & feeling
Have gathered bright & free
Round a true friend whose smile unsealing
Mirth, wit, & sympathy,
Tinged the short hours too swiftly flying
With happy life, & now
Is gone; Such home for thee is sighing
For such a friend art thou—

---

[14] Blanche Buckley corresponded with Lilian's brother John when he was a
student in Oxford, ca. 1886, and it was likely during this period that she befriended
Lilian (Dupré 30). The Galsworthy family spent their 1889 summer holiday in
Kingillie, Inverness, Scotland (Marrot 69). Blanche later became a painter (Artist
Biographies; Royal Academy of Arts 156-157).

Lilian Sauter's *Through High Windows*

The simple cover of *Through High Windows* belies the richness of its opening pages which, in themselves, reflect the arc of Lilian's life filled with curiosity about interior and exterior worlds, independence and friendship, love and sociability, and political advocacy and associations [Figure 25]. The aforementioned etching of lilies, her namesake flower, greets readers on page one [Figure 26]. Her dedication of the book follows: "To my husband," Georg, her partner in the creative, intellectual, and loving life they led in their Holland Park home. In the copy of *Through High Windows* she presented to Georg at Christmas 1911, she inscribed "We needs must love the highest when we see it," from Alfred Tennyson's *Idylls of the King* [Figure 27].

The epigraph of *Through High Windows* is a quote from Tao Te Ching, the Chinese classic text and foundational work of Taoism by the philosopher Laozi who lived during the 4th century BC: "A man may know the World without leaving his own home. Through his windows he can see the Supreme...". Several years after the publication of *Through High Windows*, Lilian's sister Mabel translated into English Henri Borel's book, originally written in Dutch, *The Rhythm of Life: Based on the Philosophy of Lao-Tse*, suggesting the common interest of the sisters in this philosopher.

Lilian then offers her readers an overview of the publication history of the poems collected in *Through High Windows*. As the introduction of this book makes clear, there is much more to this history, and now, more than one hundred years after its original publication, we can appreciate *Through High Windows* anew along with a portrait of the life of its intriguing author.

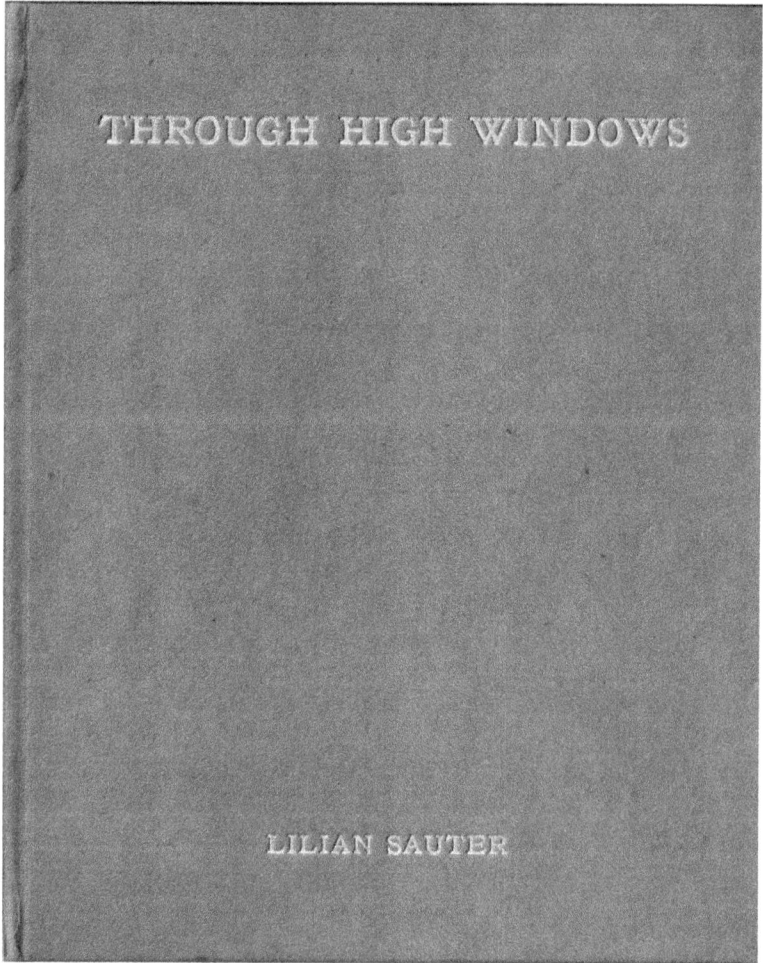

Figure 25
The cover of *Through High Windows*.
Collection and courtesy of the author.

Figure 26
Page one of *Through High Windows* depicting the same etching of lilies, Lilian's
namesake flower, which had accompanied her "Woman's Highest Plea for Suffrage"
published in leaflet form by The Women's Printing Society through an agreement
between Lilian and WWSL.
Collection and courtesy of the author.

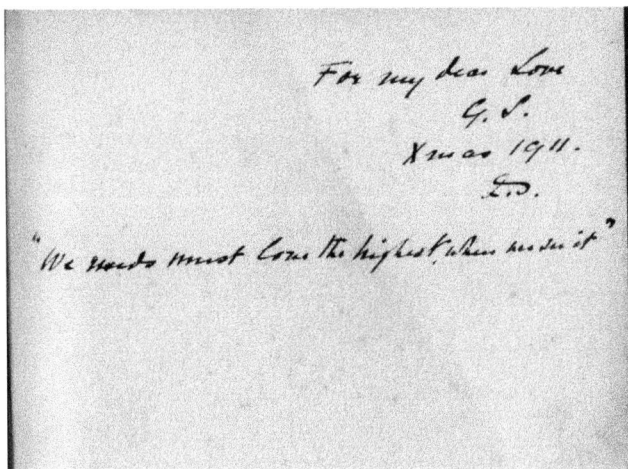

Figure 27
Lilian's inscription in an original copy of *Through High Windows* presented to her
husband Georg: "We needs must love the highest when we see it," from Alfred
Tennyson's *Idylls of the King*.
Courtesy of University of Delaware Libraries.

"A man may know the World without leaving his own home. Through his windows he can see the Supreme…."

From the Tao-Teh-Ching—King of Laotze.

TO MY HUSBAND

My thanks are due to the Editor of the English Review for permission to reprint "The Aviator" and "The Pause"; and to the Editor of the English-woman for permission to reprint "Trevone," "Astrantia," "To Love," "Storm-Cry," "Still life," and "Woman"; and to the Editor of the Vineyard for permission to reprint "Poet's Work."

I also wish to thank the Women Writer's Suffrage League for kindly allowing me to include "Woman's Plea for Suffrage" in this volume.

CONTENTS

TREVONE

SONG I. MINOR KEY

Gray hills, low rocks, blurred sea with fringe of spray,
Gray sky, gray birds, and winds all winged with gray
Of sea mists flying,

> Speak in low music to my heart,
> Of some dim world where I have part
> With things undying.

August 1907.

TREVONE

SONG II. MAJOR KEY

In purple pools, half dry,
The great rocks lie,
Huge monsters sunning in their tranquil home.
In from the clear green sea
Rolls ceaselessly
Ridge upon ridge of white-tossed, thundering foam.

Beneath the blue how swift
The gay winds shift
Their gleaming colour over pool and bay!
Through all the limpid sky
The winged clouds ply,
And drop their purple shadows from the gray.

Wonder of motion, wonder!
Eternal thunder
Of elements that ever war and weave
World-rhythms, our hearts know
Your beat and flow—
O music greater than our songs achieve!

August 1908.

THE EARTH SPEAKS

Bend low your ear, my music passes.
Fresh from the mountains, clear and keen,
My wind blows through the pines close clinging,
Blows through the valleys warm and green,
With all their sweetness filled goes singing,
And sighing through the slender grasses.

Lay your head here upon my breast,
Unbind your heart, slip off all care,
Loose the strung nerves, let be all willing,
In my cool, hushed, and tender air
The throb of fevered pulses stilling,
And let your world-worn spirit rest.

Schynige Platte,
19th August 1910.

ASTRANTIA

Pale ashen flower, of petals alpen-gray,
Whose crater holds a heart of liquid rose,
Or purple pale, as grasses ripe for hay,
A heart of flowerets tinged like evening snows.
Flower ethereal, incandescent, strange!
Compounded of the rocks wherefrom you spring,
And of the light, whose crowning rubies change
To amethyst, and of the mists that fling
Their gray upon the mountain's flaming brow,
Thou—as thy stem of slender strength upholds thee,
Star chalice, on the hill's high altar—thou
Art one with all the wonder that enfolds thee,
Symbol, thy cup, of life's twin mystery,
A heart of flame in a gray world to me!

21st August 1909.

STORM-CRY

The mountains blacken; deep, and deeper grows
The valley's purple! Vaporous dragons loom
Insurgent, swoop, and circle round the snows,
And streaks of flame tear the engulphing gloom.
You elements unbridled, yet controlled,
Hurl! hurl your rains, and fling afar your fire!
You voices peal, from peak to peak! you cold
Winds lash my spirit! Sting my swift desire!
Unmask, unshackle, set my spirit free!
Take in thy multitudinous embrace—
Great Universe of fierce immensity—
My utmost being! Strangle and efface
These elements of self that fetter me,
And hold my will clenched to the heart of thee!

16th August 1909.

STILL LIFE

In this high rock-crowned vale the air is still,
Around the peaks the white mists creep and climb,
The water murmurs, welling from the hill,
And on the far green slope the cow-bells chime.
Soft rain, hushed wind, amid the rocks a whirr,
A flash of orange flame and swift brown wings,
And in the grass, the gentle, living stir
Of myriad little unregarded things.
The bells of blue that gem the gleaming grass,
The studs of burnished gold, and ruby rose,
The pale gray rock; and high, beyond the pass,
The silent region of unruffled snows;
All still, all living, bird and flower, and hill!
In this high vale, the greatest is most still!

30th August 1909.

ETERNAL SNOWS

Great altars of the world, high snows serene,
Reared in the infinite clarity of space!
Regions of peace, unfathomed! unforeseen!
How warm the valleys glow around the base!
There the light dances on the flower-starred grass,
And the lake gleams, and life is young and gay!
Thence wanderers travel up the rock-barred pass,
Toil-worn and foot-sore through the burning day.
As through the day of life, so here they strain,
By steep ways groping through the forest's shade
Up by wild rocks through storms of numbing rain,—
Wild ways of sorrow,—eager, unafraid
To pass your far chill mists, and passing cease
Their toil, and enter your eternal peace.

15th August 1909.

TO J.N.[15]

Friend, I have wished you here these many days,
Your foot beside me, and your spirit with mine!
When wandering by the sweet wild mountain ways,
Where fresh winds blow the sun-warmed scents of pine.
Where, in fine woven blue and purple stand
The mountains; and the valleys, silver-green,
Are gemmed with precious blue, as by your hand
Silk robe with blue beads broidered I have seen!
For in this beauty of the earth and sky,
Glory of purple, green, and blue, displaying
A never ceasing rhythm of pageantry,
Is the great Self of All, herself arraying;
And we too joy with her, for we are even
Children of earth and of the Starry Heaven.

August 1909.

[15] Jessie Newbury (1864-1948), Scottish artist and embroiderer, whom Lilian
mentions periodically in contemporary diaries and letters (Cadbury Library,
JG(II)/9/1 and 10/1).

TO G.S.[16]

Thy spirit has the candour of the snows,
The bridal clearness of the mountain dawn,
Where the high thought to finest issue grows,
And Nature's force with every breath is drawn.
Thy soul is mated with the mountain storm!
Swift in its onset, strenuous, fierce, and free.
Yet, like the rock's indomitable form,
It fronts alone the winds of destiny.
The flame of heaven glowing in the West
Is not more warm and tender than thy heart,
Like Alpenrosen on the mountain's breast,
Rock-rooted, firm in Nature's clasp thou art!
To thee her deepest, her most sacred things
In the soft darkness of the night she brings.

8th September 1909.

---

[16] Georg Sauter.

HEART-LIGHTED

The night has hung her leaves so low
   Beneath her gold-domed air!
Like amber lamps they swing and glow,
   And all the world is fair:
   Why is the world so fair?

Because too full my heart is filled
   With joy,—like golden light—
And over all the world 'tis spilled;
   O joy-lit heart burn bright!
   My love comes home to-night!

31st October 1910.

TO B.C. O'S.[17]

Sea, whose ripples veil
    A depth untold,
Night, whose lamps make pale
    Her stars' rare gold,

Wind, light-fingered breeze,
    Whose touch is mirth,
Yet can move deep seas!
    Can hold the earth!

Things of hidden might
    Are in my mind
Friend with you,—dear Night—
    Deep Sea, brave Wind!

Church House, 1911.

---

[17] Elizabeth Curtis O'Sullivan (1865-1953), American painter. Lilian's son Rudolf and Elizabeth's son Curtis were school friends (Reznick 80, 108).

POETS WORK

To pluck a thought out from the heart of life,
Plunge it in molten words, and fling it high!
A flaming banner in the gloom of strife,
A beacon blazing in a storm-swept sky.

To cull the tender things of life that grow
Unseen, and set them in an honoured place,
That those who tread them under foot may know
The flower-like gems of gentleness and grace.

Through all the intricate ways of life to hold
The one straight thread that leads to higher planes,
That fine-spun rectitude, whose cobweb gold
Outweighs the weight of all life's grosser gains.

To see beneath the maze of sensuous things
A beauty that evades, a mystery
That lifts life's comedy, a hope that brings
Light to the deepest depth of tragedy.

Not—dreaming only of past days—to pour
Oil on old embers; for life's fire burns still
Clear, as of old for Greek or Troubadour,
New lamps are ours with living flame to fill.

There is no theme but beauty for the singer!
Beauty distilled from life, and wrung from pain
Is song's most sacred burden, and the bringer
Of the more noble, more enduring gain.

3rd March 1910.

THE AVIATOR

O God! To have the world beneath our feet!
To mount and glide and soar and looking down
Upon the little men that dot the street,
And all the tiny tracing of the town,

For once to measure with an infinite span
The petty things of earth, from heaven's great height,
And thence to view the works and ways of man,
And judge their values with a clearer sight!

O Joy! To race the winds and hear their singing,
To cleave the clouds, and spring, and swoop, and rise,
And on and on in the infinite up-winging,
With throbbing pulse and sun-confronting eyes,

To soar, alone, above, in the immense
Blue freedom of the sky, where time and space
Dissolve in joy of motion, and the sense
Of power out-runs the little earthly race

Of creeping men—O God! What joy of fine
New being this! Shall not our race grow fair
With powers like these? Greater, more free, divine
From kinship with the all-transcending air.

8th March 1910.

LONDON SPRING

Sing, sing, 'tis Spring!
   Little buds of crystal, spray
   The dancing breeze,
   Little flames of green burn gay
   On all the trees,
   Slender threads of brown and white
   Make mystic weaving,
   Through soft films of opal light
   Dark wings are cleaving.
Sing, Sing, 'tis Spring!
   Mats of blue the scillas spread,
   Dear daffodils
   Lay their gold for us to tread,
   And jacinth bells
   And crocus trumpets blow and ring
   Their silent mirth,
   And almond trees their rose-rain fling
   To brushing earth.
Sing, sing, 'tis Spring!

6th April 1907.

EASTER MORNING

Over London's Winter trees'
Delicate black traceries
Light is spinning golden threads,
Hanging every tip with beads,
Almond-blossom glimmers through,
All is wrapt in veils of blue.

Morning's magic, spells of Spring
Touch to splendour everything!
Weave a tissue fine and rare,
Flush of bloom in film of air,
Like some broidery faint and old,
Amethyst and pearls and gold.

31st March 1907.

STREETS OF GOLD

Night is washed Autumn rain,
Acrid scents in the air cling cold!
Black the shadows, sharp as pain!
London streets are paved with gold!

High and dark the dome of night,
Brazen dome, all dim and old,
Golden-lined with powdered light!
For the streets are paved with gold!

Rhythmic roll of traffic beats,
Pleasure calls to young and old—
Lays the lure of lighted streets—
Wondrous streets all paved with gold!

Here a child with wind-blown hair
—Heaven is dark, the wind blows cold!—
Waits to cross, her feet are bare,
But the streets are paved with gold.

Women, still, with hungry eyes,
Waiting in the shadow, hold
Paltry wares for sale, who buys?
Though the streets are paved with gold!

Men and women, moth-like, gray,
Haunt the lights, for homes are cold!
Drink, to drown their dreary day,—
Yet the streets are paved with gold!

Shadows! shadows! Let them be!
Life's aflame though hearts be cold!
Starve and suffer, what care we?
London streets are paved with gold!

SOVEREIGNTY

Great arch! Through which kings pass alone.
Grave thing of stone!
Firm, central, in a human sea,
Symbol to me
Of that impending royal gate
Where, isolate,
Each soul goes forth a king in the last hour!

Altar of waning social creeds!
Our human needs
Send clamour ringing through the night,
Of the aimless fight
And crush of men unled, the vain
Mad rush for gain,
And all the forging of the people's power.

It pales, our State's proud ritual!
A newer call
Thrills all our life; the clarion—
Not all for one,
But one for all! Yet that great thing
Which makes a king
Remains, the will's imprisoned sovereignty.

So, to the purple of the sky
Bear thy head high!
The lights shall lay on thee their gold,
The mists unfold
Their incense, life's procession raise
Its song of praise,
Till each man passing, feels: The King am I!

Autumn 1909.

TO LOVE

Wings of fugitive fire!
Deep desire of my dream!
Flower of the seed of desire!
Heart of the flower supreme!

Rhythm of beating wings!
Life from a dream unfurled!
Vision of unseen things
Held in the heart of the world!

All have come with the years!
These, and the power to hold
Deep welled, even thy tears,
O heart of the flower of gold!

Berlin,
25th November 1909.

THE PAUSE

Surely our life, in essence, is concrete
Eternal verity, and death
Only the pause in the incessant beat
Of many-pulsing life, the breath
Indrawn, the wave receding, that returns?

Not the eternal dark which severeth,
Not quenching of the light that burns,
Only a moment's holding of the breath,
A moment's darkening of the sight,
A hush, a step, the unknown openeth...

On the alternate wave-beat of the light? ...

12th March 1910.

WOMAN

Far travel the gleams of her glory,
Dim message from Matriarch days,
Linked legends in stone and in story
Still tell of her queendom, and praise
    Her the Mother and maker of men.

O'er ages of war and rude clamour
Her gentleness, spreading white hands,
Has litten a beauty and glamour
Of worship through all the dim lands,
    Ave Mother of God! and of men!

But slow, with the death of old chivalry,
Grows with a civilized age
The Ascendance of man, and a rivalry,
Limiting, building the cage
    For the handmaid and mistress of men!

There falls but a trail of her splendour
To light the dark days of despair,
To embitter her hours of surrender,
A longing to do and to dare,
    In the drudge and the plaything of men.

So, deep in her apathy, folding
Weak wings of resistance, to wait,
Fulfilling her destiny, moulding
Her mind for the needs of the state,
    She is learning the measure of men!

Low, low, where her spirit lies glowing,
Strong winds of the will to be free
Sweep over her; blowing—blowing—
O wind from the land of "to-be"
    Blow! blow! for the waking of men!

Sweet wind of the dawn of endeavour
Brings in the white day of new fame.

From sleep she emerges for ever,
Springs forth as a bird, as a flame!
   Enkindling the courage of men.

Hail! hail to her full revelation!
No queen and no slave shall she be!
But strong for the weal of the nation
A voice shall be hers with the free!
   Acclaim her the comrade of men!

WOMAN'S PLEA FOR SUFFRAGE

It is no favour, and no charity,
No ease, and no exemption from the strife
We ask, but only this—to live
Freed from a state-imposed disparity,
With all our powers, and to the full our life.
We claim the right to serve—to give.

Were it a passing whim, a mean desire,
A boon for self we craved, then might we blush
In asking, you in offering!
But we are come with heart and will on fire
To serve, moved onward by the vast slow crush
Of multitudes in suffering.

When our land boasts of freedom, this is shame,
That more than half our great community,
Unvoiced, be forced in devious ways,
By private influence to urge its claim
On those who flout it with impunity
For that subservience they praise.

Not on our wrongs or rights we take our stand,
Not make appeal from wounded vanity,
On ground above sex-variance,
On Right itself we 'stablish our demand,
On justice, and on that humanity
Which is our joint inheritance.

Could you dam back the mountain torrent's flow
Or chain the tides, or furl the force of Spring,
Then you might stem the flood of life
That bears us on from simple forms, and low,
From unity through difference, to wring
High harmony from dual strife.

That angel sex, that at the very source
Of the world's life sits, troubling all its stream

With turmoil of sweet difference,
Is deathless. Fear not! Life shall hold its course!
But in life's intricate, evolving scheme
One thread is clear to our dim sense;

This: in life's lowest glimm'rings parenthood
Is but a passing care, as life grows fine
Grows care for child, and race, till late,
And at the highest height of human good
It calls on man and woman to combine
In nurture of their child, the State!

Be ours the sphere of home, our highest call
To bear and mould the race; be yours the care
For sustenance and strength combined,
We have our work apart, you yours, but all
Have human powers beyond, with which to share
In the great service of mankind.

Therefore, by Nature's laws, and by the need
And duties they impose, and by the heart
That lights all hope for larger good,
By your integrity, and ours who plead,
We claim enfranchisement to bear our part,
The part of larger Motherhood!

WOMAN'S SONG OF FREEDOM

Raise the song of liberation!
Rouse the fire in every heart!
For the weal of all the nation!
Women claim their equal part!
    Raise the song of freedom!

Call the low land and the valleys,
Wake the wide and wind-swept hills,
Voice the slums and crowded alleys,
In the work-room and the mills
    Breathe the song of freedom!

Lift the heart to high endeavour,
Fire the thought, and nerve the will,
Though the bonds be hard to sever
Clasp your faith in justice still!
    Break the way for freedom!

Like a wide and flowing river,
Rolling onward to the sea,
Woman's life shall deepen ever!
O thou River wide and free!
    Bear us on to freedom!

On to larger duty, flinging
Wide the mother-heart to all!
Till the nations hear our singing,
Till they answer freedom's call
    Raise the song of freedom!

January 1911.

(Set to music by Annette Hullah)

Works Cited and Consulted

Archival Sources, arranged by holder

The British Library
Collection of Jeremy Jay and The Othona Community
Collection of Robert and Jane Oldmeadow
Leeds Art Gallery, Artwork of Georg Sauter
Library of Congress, Digital Collections
Liss Llewellyn Fine Art
London School of Economics, Annual Reports of the London
    Society for Women's Suffrage, 1907-1913
Bishopsgate Institute Archives and Special Collections, London
    Ethical Church Archive. Annual Reports of the West London
    Ethical Society, 1898-1901; 1912
National Library of Medicine, National Institutes of Health
National Portrait Gallery, Digital Collections
New York Public Library, Digital Collections
Oxford University, Taylor Institution Library
    Papers of Fredrich Max Müller and Hermann Georg Fiedler
Princeton University Library, Department of Special Collections
    Papers of Harrison S. Morris
Research and Cultural Collections, University of Birmingham
    Artwork of George Sauter and Rudolf Sauter, and related materials associated
    with the papers of John Galsworthy held by Cadbury Research Library, Special
    Collections, University of Birmingham
University of Birmingham, Cadbury Research Library, Special Collections
    Papers of Georg, Valda, Rudolf, and Viola Sauter JG(II)/9 and JG(II)/12
    Papers of Lilian Sauter JG(II)/10, including pocket diaries (JG(II)/10/1, 1891-
    1924), notebooks (JG(II)/10/2, 1880-1915), leaflets/pamphlets (JG(II)/10/3),
    sketchbooks (JG(II)/10/4), address books (JG(II)/10/6), and correspondence
    (JG(II)/10/7-10)
University of California, Berkeley, The Bancroft Library
    Kathleen Norris and Charles Gilman Norris family photographs
University of Delaware Libraries
    Inscribed copy of Lilian Sauter, *Through High Windows* and collection of
    poems, autograph manuscripts and typescript, 1898-1924, including her untitled
    Christmas poem (1890), acrostic poem "Painting in Venice" (1897), "May
    Night" (ca. 1908), "Frieda," "Prayer for Frieda," and "To Viola" (August 1924).
The University of Sheffield Library, Special Collections and Archives
    Papers of George Devey
The University of Texas at Austin, Harry Ransom Humanities
    Research Center, Edward Gordon Craig Collection, 1878-1973
Wellcome Collection, Digital Collections

Published Sources

"A Beautiful Character." *Evening Standard* (30 October 1924), 4.
"Approaching Marriages." *East Anglican Daily Times* (16 July 1894), 4.
Black, Helen C. *Pen, Pencil, Baton and Mask: Biographical Sketches with Six Portraits.*
    London: Spottiswoode, 1896.
Borel, Henri; translated by M.A. Reynolds *The Rhythm of Life: Based on the Philosophy of*
    Lao-Tse, translated by M.A. Brentano's: New York, 1921.

Curtis, Adela. *The New Mysticism: Six Lectures Given in Kensington, and at Cobham, Surrey*, London: Curtis and Davison, 1906.

Earle, Marie Theresa Villiers. *A Third Pot-Pourri*. Smith, Elder & Co., 1903.

Edersheim, Alfred. *Den Heliga Historien*. Stockholm: Fosterlands-stiftelsens förl.-exp., 1896.

"*The English Review.*" *The Globe* (31 August 1910), 5.

"Fire Outrage at Kew Gardens—New Tea Pavilion Burned to the Ground." *The Daily Mirror* 21 February 1913, 3.

Furst, Herbert. "George Sauter… An Impression." *The Art Record* 2, no. 41 (January 1902), 665.

"Germans Who May Stay." *The Globe* (January 16, 1919), p. 9.

Gomersall, W.J. *Westminster Review* 166, no. 1 (July 1906), 114.

"Honorary Associates' Subscriptions." *Jus Suffragii: The International Woman Suffrage News* (April 1, 1917), 96.

"Honorary Associates' Subscriptions." (April 1, 1918), 115.

Hullah, Annette. *A Little History of Music*. London: E. Arnold., 1911.

———. *Theodor Leschetizky*. London: J. Lane Co., 1906.

"The International Women's Relief Committee – I." *Jus Suffragii: The International Woman Suffrage News* (November 1, 1914), 193-4.

Kitson, Richard. "*The Musical World* (1866-1891): The Richter Concerts." *The Musical World*. (12 June 1886), 381. https://ripm. org/?page=JournalInfo&ABB=MWO

"Mr. Galsworthy's Loss." *The Nottingham Evening Post* 3 November 1924, 4.

"The Magazines." *The Common Cause* (July 7, 1910), 208.

"Militancy for Non-Militants: A Spiritual Militancy League." *Votes for Women* (21 February 1913), 301.

"A New League: The Woman's Charter," *The Devon and Exeter Gazette* (18 March 1913), 2.

"Orange and Black, Manifesto by 'Spiritual Militants, Appeal to Clergyman," *London Standard* (March 17, 1913), 11.

A. J. R., ed. *The Suffrage Annual and Women's Who's Who, 1913*. London: Stanley Paul & Company, 1913. 134-7.

"Recent Verse." The Guardian (13 March 1912), 5.

Rhoades, James. *Wedding Rhymes*. London: Curtis and Davison, 1912.

Robins, Elizabeth. *Way Stations*. London: Hodder and Stoughton, 1913.

Royal Academy of Arts. *The Academy Notes*. London: Wells, Gardner, Darton and Company, 1904.

Royal Blue Book: Fashionable Directory and Parliamentary Guide, January 1899. Kelly's Directories Limited, 1899.

Sauter, Lilian "The Aviator." *The Argonaut* (6 January 1912), 10.

———. "The Aviator." *The English Review* 6 (September 1910): 193-194.

———. "The Aviator." *Jackson Daily News* (14 January 1911), 3.

———. "The Aviator." *The Living Age* (12 November 1910), 386

———. "The Aviator." *The Province* (5 November 1910), n.p.

———. "Estrantia." [sic] *The Englishwoman* 5, no. 14 (1910), 199.

———. "Estrantia." [sic] *The Woman Worker* 4, no. 39 (1910), 834.

———. "The Pause" and "The Aviator." *The English Review* 6 (September 1910): 193-194.

———. "The Poet's Work" *The Vinyard* 2 (September 1911), 511.

———. "Still Life." *The Englishwoman* 7, no. 21 (1911), 267.

———. "Trevone." *The Englishwoman* 5, no. 14 (1910), 199.

———. "To Love." *The Englishwoman* 5, no. 15 (1910), 262.

_____. "Storm Cry." *The Englishwoman* 6, no. 18 (1910), 264.
_____. "Woman." *The Englishwoman* 9, no. 26 (1911), 188.
Smithes, Marion F. *Children of the Desert*. London: Curtis and Davison, 1910.
"Spiritual Militancy League for the Women's Charter of Rights and
      Liberties." *The Vote* (May 2, 1913), 15.
"Suffragette Incendiaries: Wearing Men's Clothes They Burn Pavilion
      in Kew Gardens." *The Gazette* (21 February 1913), 1.
"Suffragists Burn a Pavilion at Kew." *The New York Times* (21 February 1913), 5.
"*Through High Windows.*" *The Poetry Review* 5 (May 1912), 234.
"The Weddings of the Week: Mr. George [sic] Sauter to Miss B.L.
      Galsworthy." *The Gentlewoman* (11 August 1894), 170.
"The Women Writers' Suffrage League." *The Common Cause* (October
      26, 1911), 508.
"The Women Writers' Suffrage League." *The Referee* (October 29, 1911), 1.
"The Women Writers' Suffrage League." *The Vote* (October 28, 1911), 4.
"The Women Writers' Suffrage League." *Votes for Women* (October 27, 1911), 63

Secondary Sources

Amigoni, David. *Life Writing and Victorian Culture*. New York: Routledge, 2006.
Barker, Dudley. *The Man of Principle: A Biography of John Galsworthy*. New York: Stein
      and Day, 1970.
"Buckley Helen Blanche 1860-1953." *Artist Biographies*. https://www.artbiogs.
      co.uk/1/artists/buckley-helen-blanche. Accessed November 5, 2024.
"Chiswick Press and The Chiswick Shakespeare." *Chiswick Book Festival. Writers Trail.*
      https://www.chiswickbookfestival.net/chiswick-timeline-writers-trail/
      chiswick-press-and-the-chiswick-shakespeare/. Accessed November 2,
      2024.
Crawford, Elizabeth. *The Women's Suffrage Movement: A Reference Guide 1866-1928*.
      New York: Routledge, 2003.
Dupré, Catherine. *John Galsworthy: A Biography*. New York: Coward, McCann &
      Geoghegan, 1976.
Eustance, Claire, et al., eds. *Suffrage Reader: Charting Directions in British Suffrage History*.
      Bloomsbury Academic, 2000.
Farr, Maria. "Maria Theresa Earle," *Exploring Surrey's Past*, https://www.
      exploringsurreyspast.org.uk/wp-content/uploads/2021/03/Maria-
      Theresa-Earle-draft-by-Miriam-Farr-for-ESP-Di-edit.pdf. Accessed
      November 15, 2023.
Fréchet, Alex. *John Galsworthy: A Reassessment*. Totowa, New Jersey: Barnes and Noble
      Books, 1982.
Gianfaldoni, Serena, et al. "History of the Baths and Thermal Medicine." *Macedonian
      Journal of Medical Sciences* 5, no. 4 (July 2017): 566-568.
Gindin, James. *The English Climate: An Excursion into a Biography of John Galsworthy*.
      Ann Arbor: University of Michigan Press, 1979.
_____. *John Galsworthy's Life and Art: An Alien's Fortress*. London: Palgrave
      Macmillan, 1987.
Harvey, Charles, and Jon Press. "The Ionides Family and 1 Holland Park." *Decorative
      Arts Society Journal* 18 (January 1994): 2–14.
Hellerstein, Erna Olafson, et al., eds. *Victorian Women: A Documentary Account of
      Women's Lives in Nineteenth-Century England, France, and the United States*.
      Stanford: Stanford University Press, 1981.
"Holland Park." *Historic England*. http://www.imagesofengland.org.uk/details/
      default.aspx?id=480017. Accessed 30 June 2021.

"Household Books Published in Britain." University of California, Davis. http://householdbooks.ucdavis.edu/authors/2326. Accessed 30 June 2012.

"James McNeill Whistler: The Etchings, A Catalogue Raisoneé: Alexander Constantine Ionides, 1810-1890." University of Glasgow College of Arts. https://etchings.arts.gla.ac.uk/catalogue/biog/?nid=IoniAC. Accessed 28 December 2020.

Kent, Susan Kingsley. *Sex and Suffrage in Britain, 1860-1914*. Princeton: Princeton University Press, 2014.

Knoester, M.W. "Faith of a Novelist: Religion in John Galsworthy's Work." 2006. Leiden University, PhD dissertation. Leiden University Scholarly Publications, https://hdl.handle.net/1887/4303.

Kraditor, Aileen S. *The Ideas of the Woman Suffrage Movement, 1890-1920*. New York: Columbia University Press, 1965.

Marrott, Harold Vincent. *The Life and Letters of John Galsworthy*. London: Heinemann, 1935.

Mayhall, Laura E. Nym. *The Militant Suffrage Movement: Citizenship and Resistance in Britain, 1860-1930*. Oxford: Oxford University Press, 2003.

Mottram, Ralph Hale. *For Some We Loved: An Intimate Portrait of Ada and John Galsworthy*. London: Hutchinson, 1956.

Nelson, Carolyn Christensen. *Literature of the Women's Suffrage Campaign in England*. Peterborough, Ontario: Broadview Press, 2004.

Oldfield, Sybil. *International Woman Suffrage*. London: Routledge, 2003.

Park, Sowon S. "The First Professional: The Women Writers' Suffrage League." *Modern Language Quarterly* 58, no. 2 (1997): 185-200.

Reynolds, Mabel. E. *Memories of John Galsworthy*. R. Hale & Company, 1936.

Reznick, Jeffrey S. *War and Peace in the Worlds of Rudolf H. Sauter: A Cultural History of a Creative Life*. London: Anthem Press, 2022.

Ruedy, Ralph Herman. "*Ford Madox Ford and the* English Review." 1976. Duke University, PhD dissertation. Modernist Journals Project. https://modjourn.org/wp-content/uploads/2019/02/Ruedy.pdf.

Ruth, Janice E., and Evelyn Sinclair. *Women of the Suffrage Movement*. Washington, DC: Pomegranate, 2006.

Sauter, Rudolf H. *Galsworthy the Man: An Intimate Portrait*. London: Owen, 1967.

Sheppard, F. H. W., Ed. *Survey of London* 37, Northern Kensington. London: London County Council, 1973.

Small, Ian. "Special Collections Report: The Galsworthy Collection and Its Fate." *English Literature in Transition, 1880-1920* 27, no. 3 (1984): 236-238.

Stalla, Bernhard Josef. *Lebenswege eines Malers und Zeichners: George Sauter*. Brannenburg: Peter Drexler, 2011.

Stibbe, Matthew. *Civilian Internment during the First World War: A European and Global History, 1914-1920*. New York: Palgrave Macmillan, 2019.

Tickner, Lisa. *The Spectacle of Women: Imagery of the Suffrage Campaign 1907-14*. Chicago: University of Chicago Press, 1988.

Williams, Dane A. "He, She, They, Other: An Examination of Gender Associations with the Chatelaine in the Anglo-Saxon Culture." 2022. University of Montana, PhD dissertation. ScholarWorks. https://scholarworks.umt.edu/etd/11941.